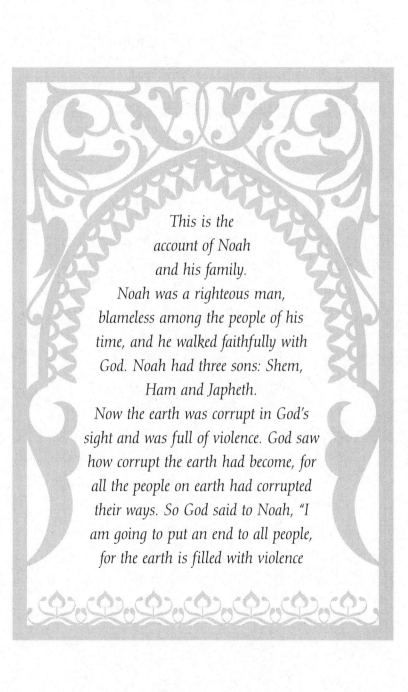

This is the
account of Noah
and his family.
Noah was a righteous man,
blameless among the people of his
time, and he walked faithfully with
God. Noah had three sons: Shem,
Ham and Japheth.
Now the earth was corrupt in God's
sight and was full of violence. God saw
how corrupt the earth had become, for
all the people on earth had corrupted
their ways. So God said to Noah, "I
am going to put an end to all people,
for the earth is filled with violence

because of them. I am surely going to destroy both
them and the earth. So make yourself an ark of
cypress wood; make rooms in it and coat it with
pitch inside and out. This is how you are to build
it: The ark is to be three hundred cubits long, fifty
cubits wide and thirty cubits high. Make a roof
for it, leaving below the roof an opening one cubit
high all around. Put a door in the side of the ark
and make lower, middle and upper decks. I am
going to bring floodwaters on the earth to destroy
all life under the heavens, every creature that has
the breath of life in it. Everything on earth will
perish. But I will establish my covenant with
you, and you will enter the ark—you and your
sons and your wife and your sons' wives with
you. You are to bring into the ark two of all living

creatures, male and female, to keep them alive
with you. Two of every kind of bird, of every kind
of animal and of every kind of creature that moves
along the ground will come to you to be kept alive.
You are to take every kind of food that is to be eaten
and store it away as food for you and for them."
Noah did everything just as God commanded him.

—Genesis 6:9–22 (NIV)

Ordinary Women of the BIBLE

✦

A MOTHER'S SACRIFICE: JOCHEBED'S STORY *Moses*
THE HEALER'S TOUCH: TIKVA'S STORY *Bleeding Woman*
THE ARK BUILDER'S WIFE: ZARAH'S STORY *Noah*

Ordinary Women of the BIBLE

THE ARK BUILDER'S WIFE
ZARAH'S STORY

TRACY HIGLEY

Guideposts

Danbury, Connecticut

Ordinary Women of the Bible is a trademark of Guideposts.

Published by Guideposts Books & Inspirational Media
100 Reserve Road, Suite E200
Danbury, CT 06810-5212
Guideposts.org

Cover and interior design by Müllerhaus

Cover illustration by Brian Call and nonfiction illustrations by Nathalie Beauvois, both represented by Deborah Wolfe, LTD.

Typeset by Aptara, Inc.

Printed and bound in the United States of America

10 9 8 7 6 5 4 3 2 1

Ordinary Women of the BIBLE

❖

THE ARK BUILDER'S WIFE

ZARAH'S STORY

CHAPTER ONE

A chill breeze tunneled through the courtyard of the small temple, a hint of the coming darkness. The sun had dipped below the roofline of the moon god's temple nearly an hour ago. In the courtyard, those who spread their goods for sale on rough blankets and the half walls surrounding the sandy square were packing up what was left after a day of bartering.

And yet still Zarah waited, leaning against the wall as she had done for hours. Fingers playing over the smooth stones of her latest piece, ruby-red clusters set in delicate metalworking of silver, a piece as valuable as any she'd ever made.

She waited for Barsal, who had promised her four shekels for her finest work. Barsal, who flaunted his many cattle and his many children with equal pride and could well afford to pay for a necklace such as this.

Across the courtyard, a woman and her husband tied the last of their remaining leather goods into pouches strapped to a snorting donkey. The husband's hand rested lightly at the small of his wife's back as she closed the final pouch, and Zarah's heart twisted a tiny bit at the tender gesture.

Where was Barsal? Zarah scanned the street beyond the courtyard but saw only shoppers and merchants hurrying along ahead of the night.

The light was fading fast now, and it was already beyond the time of safety for traveling home, especially if she still carried the necklace. A woman alone in the dark in the city of Kish was likely to never see home again.

Not only Kish. Zarah pushed away the memories of the larger city Tikov, as evil a place as this city, even if the evil was cloaked in a veil of beauty.

The couple had finished packing up and walked their donkey across the courtyard. The woman nodded to Zarah as they passed. It was courtesy only. Zarah had few friends in this city, and hadn't for years now.

Barsal's wife, for whom she had made the ruby necklace, had once been a friend, but she had not seen her in years.

The couple slowed. "Not going home yet? It is getting late." The husband's brows drew together in judgment.

She shook her head. "Waiting for a promised customer. I'm certain he won't be long."

The man shrugged and they moved on, arm in arm. The wife leaned her head against his shoulder briefly.

Zarah sighed and looked away. She remembered what it felt like to be a true partner to her husband. To work alongside each other, eyes on the same goal, one in spirit. She had known that sort of marriage once. But these past years had brought many changes.

The wind shifted again, bringing with it the sharp tang of the tannery, the odor warning her again that nothing good moved at this time of day. She wrapped her tunic more tightly across her chest, the necklace gripped in tight fingers inside its folds.

Enough. She could wait no longer. The city of Kish had given itself up to lawlessness years ago, and regardless of her husband's efforts to maintain some semblance of holiness before his God, the rest of the city had embraced a culture of violence, greed, and license.

She tugged at the multicolored scrap of fabric on the waist-high wall beside her and rolled it into a ball. The fabric had held her lesser pieces, already sold, earlier in the day. The coins were safely tucked into a leather belt beneath her tunic, but they were a pittance compared to what Barsal had promised.

Promised, but not delivered.

The courtyard was entirely deserted now. She was alone with night falling. She cursed her own stupidity in staying so long. Only the deep desire to bring home such a welcome sum of money had kept her. Such a sum could buy enough lumber for weeks of building. Her contribution would be recognized and appreciated. It might not be the affection they had once shared, but gratitude was at least something.

She hurried into the street, then kept to the courtyard wall as she turned toward home. It was a long walk to the edges of Kish where she lived, between the city and the farmland beyond. Not much of their farmland was left any longer, of course. Not since *The Project* had begun.

The mud-brick houses of the street presented blank faces as she passed, but here and there through an occasional open doorway she caught a glimpse of lamps being lit and families circling their tables.

With her head down against the wind and her thoughts on home, the *smack* into a dark cloak knocked her backward and stole her breath.

"Barsal!"

He loomed over her, smelling unwashed and grinning like a man who had been drinking too much.

Zarah lifted her chin. "You are late. I waited. Waited too long."

Barsal folded bulky arms across his chest. His eyebrows lifted in derision. "I keep my own schedule, woman."

A tickle of self-protection made her push forward, skirt Barsal, and walk on. She did not like his mood.

Barsal grabbed her arm from behind and twisted her to face him. "Where do you think you are going?"

She yanked her arm from his meaty clutch. "Home to my husband. You may call there tomorrow if you are still interested."

"Ha!" Barsal's laugh was more menacing than amused. "No, I believe I will take the goods now." He pulled at that hand still hidden under her tunic. The necklace tumbled from her fingers to the dirt.

Zarah bent to retrieve it.

Barsal snatched it before she had a chance.

"Fine," she said. "You have your necklace. Please pay me, and we can go our separate ways before it gets any later. Neither of us wants to be out at night, I am certain."

Barsal held the necklace up to the dying light and examined it. "Well done, little priestess. Well done."

"Do not call me that."

Barsal chuckled. "No? Is that not what you are? Moon god priestess?"

"You know very well that I am not." She swallowed hard against the anger. Against the memories. How had Barsal learned of her past?

"Hmm." Barsal tucked the necklace into a pouch at his waist. "Perhaps no longer. Now you belong to another holy man, I suppose. But once…"

His leering smile turned her stomach. "Pay me, Barsal, and let us finish this."

"Oh, we are finished, little priestess. We are finished."

A stab of anxiety threatened her composure, and she fought to keep her head high and her voice calm. "I don't think you would want word getting out that Barsal did not pay what he owed."

Barsal laughed, his dark eyes piercing her. "And who would believe the word of a worthless woman that even the moon god Sin did not care to keep?"

Zarah took a step backward. "What do you know of it?"

He shrugged one shoulder and patted the pouch that held the necklace. "I make it my business to know things. Tikov is not so far away. I trade there often. And I ask questions."

Zarah ran a fumbling hand through her hair, then clenched her hands together to still their trembling. The temple built to honor the moon god.

Sin, or Nanna as he was sometimes called, held nothing but evil memories. "There is nothing to know. It was long ago."

"Hmm. Not so long that your husband wouldn't be curious to hear of your life there."

"I had no life there."

Barsal eyed her up and down, as though taking in her words and understanding their true meaning.

Yes, Tikov was long ago. And yes, it was not a life. More like a walking, waking death.

"Still," he hissed, "I should think the stories I heard would be good for telling around the fire, to your husband and your three sons."

She saw the scene played out before her in a flash. The four men, hearing the truth, mouths agape, eyes turning to her in condemnation.

Zarah threw her shoulders back and tried to return his menacing look, despite her inner trembling. "Enough of this, Barsal. You've had your fun. Pay me what you owe, then leave me alone."

Barsal laughed. "You don't seem to understand. My payment is my silence. That is all the payment you will receive, and more than you deserve for such a small bauble."

"I made that piece with extra care, out of my years of friendship with Etana. It is worth four shekels and you know it!"

"Ah, yes, but what is my silence worth?"

Two figures slid from a dark slot of an alley between houses. Barsal eyed them and then pushed past Zarah. "It is a time for being indoors. You would do well to hurry home."

She grabbed at his cloak and hung on. "You cannot do this, Barsal. I beg you! That money is needed."

He backed up and raised an arm over her head as though to strike her.

She loosened her grip on his cloak.

The two men who had come from the alley approached behind Barsal. They were both young, with a hungry look about them and their eyes on her.

She'd had no fear that Barsal would harm her. Only cheat her.

But these two, they looked as though they would take whatever money she did have left from the day's bargaining and leave her for dead in the street.

CHAPTER TWO

Zarah watched the two figures over the shoulder of Barsal, her hand involuntarily sliding into the folds of her tunic, fingers curling around the pouch of coins.

Barsal seemed to sense that her distress had moved from his actions to something even more sinister. He whirled to face their would-be attackers, hands fisted at his sides.

"Go home!"

Did Barsal think that the loudness of his voice would be enough to scare them?

The taller of the two jutted his chin toward Zarah. "Your wife should be off the street by now."

"She is not my wife."

Zarah's stomach clenched. The only thing more dangerous than a woman on the street at night was one who was there alone, without a protector. Women did not simply get assaulted in this city—they disappeared altogether.

The other of the men who had not spoken circled to stand behind Zarah. He was short but broad, with a stubbled chin and stringy hair.

A cold sweat chilled her skin, and she fought to keep from crumpling.

"Then you should be at home as well."

With a glance and a shrug at Zarah, Barsal pushed past the taller man and disappeared into the gloom, leaving her to the mercy of the two.

In the beat of silence that followed, she swallowed against the fear and tried to find her voice.

"Thank you." She nodded to the man still facing her. "I had begun to think he would not leave me alone. I am in your debt." She moved to walk past him.

He stepped into her path. "The streets are unsafe."

She tried to smile. "Then I will hurry home."

"Not alone."

Zarah frowned. There was nothing threatening about the words, nor the tone.

From behind her, the stubbly one spoke. "You are his wife, are you not?"

"As he said, I am not—"

"No, not Barsal. You are the shipbuilder's wife."

Zarah sucked in a breath. That was what they called him. The "shipbuilder." There were only a few who did not regard her husband's project with derision. Many even believed that it invoked the wrath of the local gods. "We have done nothing to—"

"Your husband deals justly." The taller man before her stepped aside and swept a hand toward the street ahead. "The least we can do is bring his wife home to him safely."

Zarah exhaled, but it was not time to be unguarded. The city was full of liars. She could not be certain these two truly had any regard for her family.

But she walked forward, and they followed at a respectful distance that did not feel threatening. Surely if they wished her harm they would not simply follow, would they?

She quickened her steps, past the line of mud-brick homes in the center of the city, toward the outskirts. Beyond the end of the main street, across their field, she could see the glow of her rooftop kitchen's cooking fire. One of the girls must have started the evening meal's preparation without her.

She risked a glance back to her escorts at the edge of the field.

They both drew to a stop at her look.

"I am nearly home now." She nodded. "Thank you."

She watched their eyes move upward, beyond the house and its glowing cook fire, to the hulking outline that lay beyond, barely visible now in the sinking light. The massive shape that defined everything in her life, that consumed the attention of her husband as surely as the cook fire consumed the dung chips that kept it burning.

There was nothing more to be said. She turned and hurried across the field, knowing that they would not follow.

She should have felt gratitude for the safety they had afforded her, but in truth she felt empty and heartsick, for she knew what was to come—returning home without the money that Barsal should have paid her.

Outside the house, the wooly sheep Muti greeted her with a soft *baaa*.

She stopped to wrap her arms around his thick middle and feel the scratchy softness of his wool against her cheek. "Good evening, old friend." No matter what reception she received from the family inside this house, Muti always welcomed her.

With a final pat to Muti's head, she pushed forward with resolve and opened the door.

"There you are!"

A flurry of skirts and dark hair met her just inside the door and pulled her inward. The soft glow of lamplight outlined Salbeth's petite figure, and the girl's arms went around her, clutching Zarah to herself.

The embrace was unexpected on so harsh a night, and tears welled before Zarah knew what had happened. She returned the girl's embrace. Salbeth had the smell of freshly baked bread in her hair, and Zarah breathed in the homey warmth of it.

The girl pulled back and examined Zarah's face. "I saw you from the rooftop, coming across the field. Saw those men following you." She gripped Zarah's arms. "Are you well? Did they have ill intent?"

Zarah tried to smile. "I am fine. They—they knew of our family. Seemed to have respect and wanted to see me safe."

Salbeth's expression of concern turned to frustration. "What were you doing out so late?"

Zarah shook her head. "It's nothing. Come. Is dinner prepared? The men must be hungry."

She led the way inward, wishing she could spend some time in the cool peacefulness of the leafy central garden, but instead she climbed the narrow stairs to the second floor, which was open to the dark sky just beginning to show its stars.

They were all there. Her family.

The muscular Shem, who leaped up to embrace his wife, Salbeth.

Witty and entertaining Japheth, with his loyal wife, Aris.

Ham, always eager to get something done, and the lovely but petulant Na'el.

And Noah. Zarah's husband.

None of them had met her at the door but Salbeth. The three wives of her sons were well able to cook the meal and keep the house and do all the things that once were her responsibility. Did any care enough to worry, to wonder where she had been?

Behind her, Salbeth whispered in her ear. "The men have just come in from the work. None of them know you were not at home."

Ah. And yet the knowledge that she was not missed did not feel comforting.

She took her place on the mat beside Noah, accepted the loaf of bread he passed to her, and tore a large hunk from it. The loaf had risen too high and was hollow inside. Perhaps Salbeth still had much to learn about the ways of the kitchen. She glanced at the girl, but Salbeth had already settled into the crook of Shem's arm and seemed unconcerned with the hollowness of her bread.

As Zarah would be, if she had a husband who was attentive for reasons that had nothing to do with bread.

"Well?" Noah's eyes were on her as she passed the loaf to Na'el. "Will we have funds enough for the next phase?"

So, it was already time. Time to speak of her failure. To make it clear in front of her entire family.

She ripped a piece of bread with her teeth and chewed it slowly. She felt as hollow as the bread tonight.

"He...he refused to pay me."

Noah set down the crock of wine he had been sipping. "What?"

"Barsal. He—he took the necklace. But he refused to pay me."

Noah was already getting to his feet.

Japheth pulled him back to his mat. "Father, there is nothing that can be done tonight."

Noah growled. "That man is a scoundrel. He makes money in every dishonest way he can think of, and then he thinks to cheat me?"

Zarah looked away. Barsal had cheated *her*, not Noah. But of course, it was all the same.

"We were to use those funds for the rest of the needed wood. We have only the rooftop and some interior pens to build before the ark is finished. And we are running out of time."

His words lingered in the air, his sons saying nothing.

It was well established that only Noah seemed to hear from his God. Shem, Ham, and Japheth were willing to work, willing to build, because their father housed them, fed them, clothed them. It was a family project, yes, but not because the sons believed the words of their father. Only because they relied upon his provision for them and their wives.

And Zarah? Did she believe? Believe what Noah had been saying for all the years that he had been building?

It had been easy at first, when they still had at least some friends, and grain in the fields. These past few years, though, when everything had dwindled to nothing, she had struggled to hold on to faith.

"We will go to him tomorrow," Noah was saying. "We four men." He nodded around the circle to his sons. "He will pay us what he owes."

Zarah said nothing. Would Barsal pay? He was a dangerous man to confront.

And would he speak to Noah of the truths he knew? Of her past that would make her even less significant in the eyes of her family?

CHAPTER THREE

Zarah woke to the sound of singing, somewhere beyond the walls of the room. She lay listening, then realized that the sound had only been in her dreaming and the house was as silent as death.

She lifted her head a fraction from her sleeping mat, opened one eye to glance at Noah's mat across the room.

He was already gone, not surprisingly. Off to work on The Project before the sun had fully risen.

This morning was no different than every other, nearly since the building of the ship began. They slept on opposite sides like strangers sharing a room at a wayside inn, with one of them always slipping out in the early dawn to work. There was no hostility. They had simply drifted apart as Noah became more consumed with his work.

But today, today *was* different.

Zarah pulled herself upright, the memory of last night flooding back.

Today Noah would take his sons and confront Barsal.

She would be shamed in front of them all. And worse, her husband and three sons would be challenging a man who had proven himself unscrupulous and violent.

No, not if she could help it. She tossed aside her blanket and climbed to her feet, then found her finest robes among her few belongings and readied herself for the day. A quick brush of her hair with the prized alabaster comb she'd brought from Tikov, and a cold splash of water across her cheeks.

Sometime in the night, listening to Noah's steady breathing and thinking about Barsal's threats, she had come up with a plan. But she would need to be quick, before Noah made good on his promise to trek across the city to Barsal's home and demand payment for the necklace.

The house was still. The others would all be asleep. No one bore the commitment to The Project that Noah did. Not enough to rise so early.

She slipped to the central courtyard, a square inside the house that was open to the sky, and made her way to the patch of soil where the garden herbs grew.

A series of large rocks bordered the herb garden, placed there by her own hands for beauty, but also to keep careless feet from walking across the tender plants. With a glance around to ensure she was alone, she pried one of the corner rocks up from the soil, revealing a hollow beneath.

Even on the outskirts of the city, you could not be certain of valuable items staying safe. Zarah had carved out this secret hiding place for the jewels that she bought with her earnings, stones that would be turned into pieces with even more value for her to sell in the market. Since the day her first son Japheth had taken a wife, she had kept the hiding place secret. The women were family now, yes, but they came from their own families that were not so devoted to Noah or his ship. She must be careful.

From the hollow beneath the rock, she pulled a small sack tied with a cord. Quickly, she tied the sack to a belt under her robes.

The plan she'd devised in the night was the only way to replace the money Barsal owed her, before Noah and her sons put themselves in danger to demand payment, and perhaps learned the truth about her.

Satisfied that the sack was well-hidden, she took a deep breath, crossed the courtyard, and made her way out of the house.

The sun hovered at the horizon, shooting rays like knife blades across the fields. Zarah shielded her eyes against the glare until she'd left the grassy area around the house and shifted toward the hulking monstrosity that was her husband's obsession.

The ship rose from the fields, blocking the merciless sun.

She would never get used to the sight. It would be comical if it were not the source of such hardship.

Zarah had never seen the sea. She had heard tales of it from her mother, as a young child. Her mother had grown up near the Great Sea, before traveling east to Tikov. She had often told Zarah and her three older sisters about the way the water stretched as far as eye could perceive, reflecting sunlight like a thousand jewels sparkling on its surface. Bringing ships, floating houses big enough to hold entire families.

That was long ago, before the dark days had begun for her.

And this ship before her now was large enough to hold the entire city. Large enough for a city but without a sea in sight.

She crossed the neglected field toward the ship. The familiar, rhythmic *thwump* of Noah's mallet rang through the early-morning air. He was somewhere above, from the sound of it. The smell of the bitumen tar that coated the outside of the ship lay heavy in the air.

But there at the base, near the wide door that opened like a mouth ready to swallow them all, was another figure, looking upward as well.

Zarah recognized the stooped figure at once and felt a smile play at the corners of her mouth, despite the concerns of the day.

Methuselah.

He turned, as though he sensed her coming.

"Good morning, Grandfather."

She always called him *Grandfather*, though he was no relation to her and actually father to Noah's father, Lamech, who had been gone five years already. Lamech had gone to earth before his own father, Methuselah, who seemed as though he would outlive them all.

"Good morning to you, Daughter." Methuselah pointed upward. "He has begun early again, I see."

She shrugged. "He says the time grows short. It makes him eager to finish."

Methuselah eyed her, his lips puckering. "You do not agree?"

"Agree? What do I know of it? Noah's God does not speak to me of such things."

"Noah's God?"

She hooked her arm into the old man's. "Your God as well, Grandfather. But still, I hear nothing of the future from him."

Methuselah grunted, as though displeased with her answer.

She was glad that the old man had come to observe the work. Perhaps the visit would keep Noah here, while she carried out the plan she'd devised in the night.

She tugged him toward the doorway. "Shall we go up?"

The wooden planks that led up into the ship put them onto the lowest deck, although the water cisterns in the belly of the ship could be accessed at the ends. This lowest deck was mainly a series of narrow pens where animals were to be kept.

The ramps were ingenious, really. A long ramp was built into the base, reaching to a small platform and then turning to ascend the other direction to a second platform on the middle deck before turning once more to reach the upper deck. They followed the sound of Noah's hammer upward, pausing on each platform to give the old man a chance to catch his breath. On the top deck, illuminated by the natural light of the opening all the way around the top of these walls, they found the ladder and climbed upward.

Finally, they emerged into the sunlight, onto the roof where Noah worked alone.

His back was to them, and he was stripped to the waist, already sweating in the morning heat.

Zarah watched him for a moment, the way the muscles of his back tensed just before he swung the mallet to strike the tenon of wood into the hollowed mortise of its mate.

She was watching Noah, but she realized that Methuselah was watching her, an amused and knowing smile on his lips.

She shook her head and looked away.

Noah turned then, saw them both, and rested his mallet against the frame he was building. He dipped his head in respectful greeting to the old man, then used his forearm to wipe the sweat from his brow. "What brings you so early, Grandfather?"

"I have news from the city."

Zarah inclined her head. Methuselah had said nothing of news on their way up the ramps.

Noah extended a hand to a bench built into the side of the ship.

Methuselah lowered himself carefully to the bench. Noah placed a sandaled foot on it and leaned on one knee. "What news?"

Zarah took a place on the rooftop at Methuselah's feet. She liked to sit at his feet as he told stories. It reminded her of the better days of childhood.

But Methuselah did not have a child's story to tell. The news was much darker, of more women disappearing from the city in the night.

Noah glared down at her. "Zarah was out alone toward evening yesterday. She could have been taken."

Zarah snorted. "What would anyone want with me?"

Both men stared down at her for a moment, as though she had said something odd, but then resumed their conversation.

"Does anyone have any word of these women? Of where they have been taken, or why?"

Methuselah shook his head. "Rumors only, as we have heard for years. The race of giants, north of here, bred from the most beautiful of women and those with uncommon evil. Some are saying that they have run out of women for breeding there and are venturing south to take for themselves." He shrugged. "As I said, strange rumors."

Zarah looked away, choosing to say nothing.

Noah dropped his foot from the bench and began to pace. "The world grows more evil every day. There will soon be nothing left of good in it at all."

"I fear we have already reached that point, my son."

The two men shared a look that spoke of knowledge she did not have. No doubt words they had heard from their God, who did not speak to women. At least, not to her.

"I wish I understood more," Noah said. "Had more information, about how—"

Methuselah held up a hand. "It will come, my son. In due time. For now, you must only obey."

Noah nodded. "But the funds have run dry again." He turned to Zarah. "Have our sons risen yet? We'll go soon, to get the payment owed by Barsal."

Zarah swallowed against the tightness in her throat. "It's too dangerous." From her place at his feet, she looked to Methuselah, hoping he would agree. "Four men, arriving without invitation. Barsal will see it as a challenge."

Noah's brows drew together in displeasure.

"Barsal is a proud man. He will not appreciate being bested by a woman, even if it is her husband and sons who force the issue."

"Surely he will be reasonable."

Methuselah snorted. "No one responds to reason anymore, my son."

Zarah patted the pouch beneath her robe. "My work has been selling well of late, Noah. I have loose stones that I can sell. There is no need to endanger yourselves and our sons by confronting Barsal. I will go to the market today—"

But Noah was shaking his head, arms crossed over his chest. "No. Not with this news of more women taken. I want you here, where it is safe."

Her heart sank. "Perhaps they are not taken. Perhaps they are leaving on their own."

"Is that truly what you think?"

She sighed and closed her eyes. "I do not know."

"Well, until we do know what is happening here, none of you women will be venturing alone from this house." The words were tinged with anger.

Zarah studied her hands in her lap. Sometimes it felt as though they were trapped in this evil city, sealed in their fate, as though a layer of bitumen tar coated everything they did.

Noah reached for his mallet. "Tell my sons to get up from their beds and join the work. We will go to Barsal in the midday heat when he is resting. He will learn that the family of Noah ben Lamech is not to be cheated."

CHAPTER FOUR

Noah watched Zarah and his grandfather cross the barren field from the prow of the ark. She had caught the old man's arm in her own and they walked like she was his own daughter, the affection between them evident even from this height.

Noah's hands tightened around the wide rim of wood. She showed such affection for Methuselah. Affection that he had grown accustomed to receiving himself over their many years together. But lately, she had changed. She seemed...colder toward him somehow. He had tried to understand why everything he did seemed to end up wrong. He'd asked his God to give him wisdom in the matter, but in truth God had been silent since this whole thing began.

Such specific instructions, such clarity in the Voice Noah had heard that night. He had rushed to mark down the details as they were delivered to him. The dimensions, the design, the materials.

Only eight of them would enter, with the chosen animals. The rest of all flesh destroyed.

Noah lifted his gaze to the city beyond his own fields. It was unthinkable that all of them would perish. And yet that was what the One God had said.

More unthinkable was that he alone, with his family, had been chosen to survive. Surely there were others who followed after the One God. Could all the truth passed down over generations have been lost to the world? Was he alone and his family all that was left?

For years he had fought against the growing darkness, just as his fathers had before him. But now it seemed that none of it mattered. "The Tenth," they called him. And then dismissed his words as the ranting of someone who clung to old ways when new ways were better.

Yes, Noah was tenth. Tenth in the line of eldest sons since God walked with Adam in the garden.

Adam and his son Seth had gone to earth before Noah had been born. And Enoch, Methuselah's father and the seventh from Adam, had simply disappeared one day. Methuselah insisted that his father had walked with God, walked so closely that he had somehow found a way to walk back into the Garden.

But the others, the rest of the line—Noah had been a boy and then a man as each of them in turn had gone to earth. First Seth's son Enosh, then Kenan, Mahalalel, Jared, and finally Noah's own father, Lamech, a few years ago.

Now only his grandfather, Methuselah, remained, and despite his following after the One God, it did not appear that Methuselah would be saved on the ark either. *Only eight*, God had told Noah that night. Only eight.

Methuselah heard the truth from Noah's own lips, and only smiled and nodded. "Not to worry, my boy. I suspect I will be headed somewhere better."

He spoke of the Garden, Noah knew. Since the day his father had disappeared Methuselah had believed that there was somehow a way back into the Garden. A way of complete restoration. "God makes the way," he often said. "The way back to Himself."

The two walking in the distance disappeared into the house. Noah pushed away from the prow and turned back to his work, taking up the mallet again to set the rest of the rough-cut timbers into their joints along the edge of the roof.

The days were evil and the time grew short—he felt it in his bones. God had been silent since the instructions were given, but surely He would act, and soon. How much longer could they survive in such a place? He had spoken confidently to Zarah about confronting Barsal for the cheated money, but part of him wondered if he and his sons would survive the confrontation. It had been years since anyone had enforced any sort of law in this land, and Barsal had been known to kill for lesser reasons.

But no, he must return to God's words. He and his sons would enter. His wife and his sons' wives. Eight would enter the ark. Only eight, but at least he could hold to that promise.

These were not the thoughts for today. Thankfully, his attention was diverted by the arrival of those sons. Zarah must have sent them to join the work, given their displeased expressions.

"So early, Father?" Japheth sighed. "I believe you'd have us work all night if the moon gave enough light to work by!"

"Yes, I would! You have been chosen by God to fulfill His purposes, and yet you would rather remain in your beds!"

"Perhaps some of us have wives that make our beds more… comfortable." Japheth grinned and looked to his brothers for approval.

Ham shrugged. "We are here, Father. Do not ask us to understand nor to agree. Your God does not speak to us."

Noah threw his mallet to the deck. "*Our* God, Ham! He is the God of your fathers, and regardless of what other gods this corrupted world tries to create, He is the only God. You would do well to speak with respect."

Ham lowered his head but said nothing.

Shem picked up the mallet and handed it back to his father. "Where do we work today?"

Noah sighed, took the tool from Shem's hand, and pointed toward the prow. "The roof is nearly finished there. Use the remaining wood to finish what you can, and we will get more later."

Noah went to the ramp to descend below, to the deep hold of the ark. He had no desire to work alongside his sons today.

He pushed them hard, he knew. But it was the only way. God had chosen them, but perhaps God would choose again. Others more worthy. Perhaps even now some other man was at the edge of another city, building another ark that was closer to being finished. Perhaps the floods would come before Noah and his sons could finish.

Nothing could be certain. He had learned that lesson when God had told him that everything he knew would be destroyed.

Hours later, sweat burned his eyes and the overpowering smell of the bitumen tar singed his nostrils, but still he worked at the mismatched joints in the stern where the water cisterns would provide ballast as well as water for drinking and washing. He was no craftsman. Why had God chosen him? The gaps, the ill-fitting joints—it would take only one weak spot to break open the entire vessel, and then they would all be lost.

He was pulling a thick splinter from his left thumb when the crash came.

The vibration shook the ark all the way down to the hold where he worked.

A yell went up from one of his sons—he could not be certain which—and then silence.

Noah took the ramp in bounds, leaped over each platform, and reached the roof in moments.

The blue sky and bright sun blinded him, and he cupped a hand over his eyes to locate the men.

Shem and Ham knelt over an open space on the roof, their arms extended down into the gap.

"Father!" Shem yelled and motioned with his head, both hands being occupied by his grip on Japheth, whom they were slowly lifting from the hole.

Japheth was up and out and huffing on the rooftop before Noah reached them.

"What happened?"

"The wood gave way." Shem flexed his shoulders. "Here"— he pointed—"there must have been a weak area."

Noah checked over each of his sons, beginning with Japheth. "You are unhurt?"

The three nodded, and then they each stood peering into the gaping hole. Three stalls on the upper deck were visible, with the failed lumber lying on their floor.

Noah's stomach churned. More delays. More cost.

Would they ever come to the end?

Ham was the first to turn away, shaking his head. "How much longer, Father? How much longer must we pursue this ridiculous project?" He swept an arm out toward the fields. "Our vineyards lie untended, our grain languishes. It is too late to reap a harvest this year, and then where will we be without food?" He circled back, his arms folded across his chest. "I understand that you believe—"

"Stop!" Noah took a threatening step toward Ham. "Do not speak ill of God's instruction."

Ham held up two hands, palms out. "Apologies, Father. I did not realize you cared about my opinion."

Noah turned away, breathing hard. "Fix it."

He returned below deck, still fuming.

But the anger was not for Ham. It was for himself.

Anger because he was failing his God. Anger because Zarah had grown so sad. Anger because he had not raised sons who also heard from God.

The ark was unfinished, and every day seemed to take them further from completion, not closer. Without the silver from Zarah's recent sale, they would have no supplies.

Murderer or not, it was time to force Barsal to pay them what he owed.

CHAPTER FIVE

The midday meal of bread and lentils was spread on the low rooftop table. The woven mats were in their places around the table. The four women who shared the home had each done their part and now waited for their husbands to return from the work.

But Zarah waited for more than that. Noah had said that they would go to Barsal in the midday. This plan was dangerous on more than one account.

She paced the rooftop under the heat of the sun. The four men had emerged from the bowels of the ship and were crossing the field. She could hear bits of their conversation, carried on the wind, but she did not watch them.

She was busy practicing what she would say to Noah.

She was going to convince him to take her alone to confront Barsal. And she was going to tell him everything.

Not here, not in the house with all the listening ears. She would wait until they were on their way and tell him as they walked.

He had known some of her past when he married her. Some but not all. She had told him bits of her young childhood. Then the most recent years before they met, of her life alone in Kish, working to support herself as a jeweler.

But the years between—the years that had so shaped and defined her—that life he knew nothing about. Would not have married her if he had known.

And so now she paced, counting the minutes until he climbed the steps, ate his meal, and they would set off together to the house of Barsal.

Barsal, who somehow knew more about her than her own husband.

The men came in with less than cheerful countenances and took their places on the mats in silence.

Zarah ladled the watered wine into crocks for each of them, and the women sat as well.

Clearly Noah was having one of his days. Setbacks with The Project often made him unhappy, and the rest of the family had learned to keep their silence on such days.

All but Methuselah, who had also stayed for the midday meal and had no such concern about Noah's moods.

"You're worrying again, my boy." The old man scooped a huge amount of lentils onto a crust of bread and popped the entire thing into his mouth. "I do not believe the One God wishes you to worry." The words were mumbled around the huge mouthful of food.

Zarah touched her fingers to her lips to hide her smile.

Na'el giggled.

But Noah was not amused. "You would worry too if you saw the shoddy workmanship and how far we have yet to go, with so little to work with."

Zarah felt the stab of his words, though they were not directly for her. But indirectly, every person around this table knew that since the fields went untended, her work now supplied the money needed for The Project.

The meal was hastily finished, and when Zarah stood to clean away the remains, Noah nodded to his sons. "Bring your swords. Though I would hate to have need of them."

"Noah, there is too much risk in this plan." She glanced at the other three women, hoping her words would bring them to her support. "You and our sons put yourselves in danger for a few bits of silver. When Barsal sees you coming, he may not even wait for you to arrive and speak. He will likely send men out to kill you before you reach his house."

As she expected, the eyes of all three younger wives widened. Aris clutched at Japheth's tunic.

Noah frowned but seemed to be considering her words.

She pressed in with her suggestion. "Let the two of us go alone. He will not expect an attack if he sees me with you. And his wife, Etana, she—she was once a friend." Zarah stumbled over the final few words. She could no longer call Etana a friend, not since The Project had begun and all their neighbors had shunned them.

Noah shook his head. "I would not trust that man with my wife, without the protection of my sons."

The bit of comfort she felt at his desire to protect her quickly vanished as she saw her chance lost, to tell him the truth before Barsal told him everything.

If Noah heard the truth from Barsal, he would believe she had lied to him. Deliberately deceived him so that he would marry her.

Well, perhaps she had.

And when she told him herself? What then? He spent so much time railing against the evils of the world, how would he react to know his wife had been such a part of it?

She was clutching at her robes, she realized, and forcibly pulled her fingers from the fabric. She drew closer to him and spoke softly. "Noah, I had also hoped to speak to you privately on the way."

His eyebrows rose, and he looked into her eyes for a moment. "Did you?"

Shem cleared his throat. "Father, you know I am not one to back away from a challenge. But I think in this, Mother speaks wisely. There is no need to provoke Barsal unnecessarily, and perhaps Mother can even speak sense to his wife and prevent any sort of confrontation."

Noah surveyed his family, nodded once, and took up his outer robe. "So be it. But we go now."

They walked side by side, across the field that had once been lush. Zarah let her hands play over the fallen stalks of sparse wheat that had grown without any attention this year. Along the house, the vines also had gone largely untended and the grapes rotted and fell where they grew. She had often asked Noah to let the women tend the fields, but he always refused, saying that there was no purpose in tending what would soon be gone. And besides, Salbeth, Na'el, and Aris were strong and able to help with the building. And Zarah's time was better spent in buying jewels from the merchants who traveled through, setting them in her careful metalwork, and then selling her pieces at a nice profit to the people of the city and the merchants as they traveled back the other direction.

They each had their part in God's story, Noah insisted. And farming was no longer part of it.

They walked in silence for some time, until the house and the fields were far behind them and they had entered the city. Barsal's home was on the other side, where the richest of city dwellers had built larger homes.

"So," Noah finally broke the silence between them, "you wanted to speak to me?"

She exhaled. Her mouth had gone dry, and the dust of the fields still burned in her eyes.

"Yes."

They walked again in silence a moment. Noah was not a man to rush another to speak. He was sometimes as quiet as she.

Zarah tried to breathe normally, but her chest seemed to catch with every breath, and her heartbeat raced ahead of her.

"I—I wanted to tell you why Barsal thought he could get away with not paying me for the jewelry."

"Because he is a—"

"Because he has heard things. Talk about me. News that I did not ever want you to hear." The words tumbled out in a rush. She had started now. Now she must finish it.

Noah said nothing. Patient and quiet as always.

She could not do it.

She had not sought him out at first, those many years ago. Her skills as a jeweler had brought her money and even some standing. She could survive without a husband and perhaps she even preferred it.

But the city had grown darker and more vicious. No woman was safe on her own. She'd needed a son, a brother, or a husband.

With no father to arrange a husband for her, she was left to find her own solution.

She had gone to him by herself. Waited until he worked in his fields alone. Crossed through the grain, stood quietly until he noticed her, then bowed her head in respect.

He laid aside his scythe, wiped his face with his tunic, and listened.

Listened to the story she told him, of her fears of being alone, and her skill with jewelry that could bring an income.

They were married immediately, much to the distress of his father, who insisted that Noah knew nothing about her.

And that was now the problem. He knew nothing of what she was about to tell him.

She sucked in a deep gulp of air, tried to let it strengthen her resolve, and spoke.

"Before I came to Kish. It is about my life…before."

A shout from behind them broke into her confession.

They both turned.

"Father!"

A figure flew toward them down the street, hair streaming behind.

"Aris!" Noah left her side and ran back. "What has happened?"

Zarah ran to join them.

Aris was panting, crying.

Noah gripped Aris by the arms and examined her face, which was scratched. A laceration split her lip, and a purpling bruise was swelling along her jawline.

She took a breath and looked up into Noah's face. "The ship is on fire!"

CHAPTER SIX

Noah may have been advanced in years, but he still prided himself on being strong enough to keep up with the younger Aris on the run back through the city. It was his wife, however, who slowed his progress.

"Go," she had said several times as they trotted along in Aris's wake. "I will get there eventually."

But he had stayed with her. Not because the city was unsafe—he allowed her to walk to and from the marketplace many times—but because there had been something in her eyes just before Aris had come.

But the breathless rush back to their home was not the time for questions. If they were to have any chance of saving the ark, there was no time for talk.

Noah ignored the inquiring looks from shoppers and merchants as they passed in such a hurry.

Surely Aris's run through the city and then the three of them hurrying back toward their home would be a sight that was spoken of widely, from the market to the taverns.

Noah gripped Zarah's hand and pulled her along.

When had he *not* been the talk of the city?

From the moment of his birth as Tenth, he had been part of something larger than himself, something that was becoming more disdained and discarded with each passing generation. It was as if he were himself a relic of another time. A time in which men revered and worshipped the One God. Made their sacrifices. Called upon Him for rain and sun, for food and family.

They reached the edge of the city, where the shops and close-built mud-brick houses leveled out to fields. Noah squinted into the sun as they ran. Their own fields and house still lay distant, and the ark that rose like a misplaced boulder against the horizon was too far to see anything but its shadow.

Zarah was breathless beside him. "Please, Noah, go. I will be fine."

He squeezed her hand, then released it and ran as fast as he still could toward the ark.

How could there be a fire? They were always so careful with torches when they worked inside, in the darker areas. His heart lurched at the thought of the bitumen tar that lined the inside and outside of the lower level. He had seen bitumen burn. Would the whole ark be aflame before he arrived?

How could this happen, when he was doing everything God instructed? When he was the *only* one who cared about the One God's instructions?

Each year took his city farther from the Garden. Not only his city but all the cities within knowledge. Temples to evil spirits sprang up like weeds, then grew large as trees, until the people forgot that they were the places of false worship, overshadowing the truth.

And still Noah and his fathers clung to the old ways, despite derision and disrespect.

Until one by one, the fathers had all left him, each in turn.

But though the city scorned him, it was his own father, Lamech, who had dealt the worst blow. Words whispered into Noah's ear while Lamech lay dying. Words that came back to him in the quietest hours of the night when he had to force them into silence if he was to carry on with the work God had given him.

And now, even that work was in danger.

He smelled the fire before he could even see it. The acrid tang of burning tar mixed with the homey smell of woodsmoke in an odd combination.

There, there was the fire, in the lowest part of the stern of the ark but spreading fast. With no water but what they could draw from their small well, they would never be able to extinguish it.

His three sons were already there when he arrived, huffing and angry.

Shem was using his bare hands to smack a woven cloth against the flames. Salbeth ran from the house with more blankets in her arms.

Japheth darted back and forth around Shem, eyes wide and hands held out uselessly.

"Father!" Ham ran out from inside the ark and grabbed Noah's arm. "We must rip away the burning section. We cannot find your largest blades!"

"In the cistern, near the prow." He started for the ark.

"Help him, Japheth!" Ham's authoritative voice seemed to snap Japheth from his stupor. "Na'el, grab those blankets from

Salbeth and work over here!" He jabbed a finger toward the opposite side of the fire from Shem's position.

Na'el backed away, hands held in front of her. "I don't want to get burned!" Her mouth tightened, and her dark eyes narrowed.

"Help us, woman!" Ham's anger at his wife seemed to flare as hot as the tar fire.

Noah ran for the iron saw-toothed blades he used for chopping, Japheth at his side.

Just inside the ark, he collided with Aris, nearly knocking the petite girl off her feet.

"*Oh,*" Aris grabbed an arm of each of the men. "I am sorry, Father. I was looking—"

They left her behind and ran for the stern.

Blades in hand, the two ran back through the square entrance of the ark, past Aris, and into the field. They sprinted down to the end of the ark. Orange-blue flames licked out from the charred wood like a snake's tongue.

Zarah had joined the fight while Noah was inside the ark. She worked alongside the other women, smacking at the flames with blankets. Her hair had loosened from its binding in the run across the city and swirled like flames of its own around her head.

Aris joined the women and took up the blanket fight.

Noah brushed at embers that sparked in the air and singed his beard. He could taste the tar, could taste the wood, could taste the project that had consumed his years burning to ash in front of him.

Ham pointed his brothers to one end of the burning section. "You two, work there!" He grabbed a blade from Noah's grip. "Father, you and I on this side!"

They set to work against the side of the ark. Noah hacked against wood that the fire had not yet reached. The fire heated the side of his body. Smoke burned his eyes.

Every stroke was a blow to Noah's heart. It was madness to rip away wood that was undamaged. But they could not work directly in the flames. The only way to save the ark was to slash out the burning section. And they must begin from the sides, where the fire had not touched.

Despite Noah's criticism of the ill-fitted joints and second-class workmanship, the boards did not rip easily. To poke a hole in the solid side of the ark, even with a blade, proved impossible.

Ham yelled across to his brothers. "We must start from the fire and work outward!"

The words were barely spoken when Shem leaped toward the flames, used his mallet to pry a burning board from its place. He flung it to the ground behind him.

"Be careful!" Salbeth's cry was laced with fear.

"Here!" Shem pointed his mallet at Japheth and then used it to direct him to a section near his own. "Pull that away!"

Japheth swung wildly at the burning wood. He barely missed Shem's head.

Behind Noah, Na'el screamed and stomped at the burning wreckage on the ground that threatened to light the dry grain field on fire.

God, where are You? Noah yanked and wrenched on the flaming lumber. The words echoed over and over in his head. *Where are You?*

"Japheth, take care!" From the corner of his eye, Noah saw Aris back away from the action. She wrung her hands and watched her husband swing his mallet at the flames.

The crackling of the burning wood grew louder.

Were they making progress? Noah dared not back away to take stock. Had the heat increased? Did the blackened area widen?

His arms grew heavy, and sweat ran down to sting his eyes along with the smoke. The blade seemed to double its weight in his hand. Its splintery handle dug into his slick palm. He used his forearm to wipe the sweat and ash from his eyes.

And still it burned.

The flames traveled parallel to the ground, consuming the line of bitumen that coated the lowest part of the ark. That was a blessing at least. If they had moved upward instead, the fire would have soon been out of reach of their tools.

They were all tiring. Noah could feel it, even without stopping to look at each of his family.

His thoughts flashed back to a fire he'd seen as a child. A neighbor's young son had tipped over an oil lamp and caught some bedding on fire. The flames had shot up inside the tiny house, near the window, and caught the attention of Noah's father. Seemingly as one, Noah remembered, the surrounding neighbors had emerged from houses and collected from the streets to help extinguish the flames. Water pots were carried out of homes by wives and daughters and handed to men to douse the flames. Within minutes the danger had passed.

But here, now, they worked alone. No one came from the city, though surely the smoke had them all watching by now. No neighbors joined the fight.

No, the days of any sort of compassion seemed to be gone.

They fought alone.

CHAPTER SEVEN

Z arah's throat was thick with smoke, and her chest burned. How could this be happening? After everything they had sacrificed to follow Noah's insistent lead that they build this ship?

She pulled back from the flames for just a moment, taking in her family in danger.

Shem, always charging in to any fight without a thought of his own safety, and Salbeth at his side, willing to serve in any way she could.

Ham barked commands at his brothers and even his father, always so sure that his way was best. Na'el held back, cowering away from the heat.

Japheth darted left and right, willing to help but never sticking with a plan long enough to do much good. Aris, trying to beat back the flames in the grasses, stopping to hold her hands against her head, helpless to stop the spread of the fire.

And Noah, swinging his blade like a madman, intent on saving his ship.

All this she saw in a flash, between lunges at every flame that erupted in the dry grain. The open field was like an invitation to the fire, and if it got away from them here, it would spread to the rest of the ship and even to the house. She could not let that happen.

Broken stalks of grain scratched at her bare ankles, and her sandals felt burnt through in more than once place.

Just then Shem and Japheth let out a joint yell, as a large section of lumber gave way and wrenched itself from the side of the ship, down onto their heads.

Japheth jumped away as the burning wood tumbled down, narrowly missing him.

Shem covered his head with his arms but took the brunt of the hit on his left shoulder.

The blow knocked him to the ground.

"Shem!" Salbeth was at his side in a flash.

Zarah was right behind her.

Shem lay on his back in the grain, but his eyes blinked open. He shook his head as if to clear some grogginess.

Salbeth knelt beside him.

"I—I am—unhurt."

But a gash in his shoulder welled with blood. Zarah cried out and bent to examine it.

"Here, I will tend to him."

She turned her head to find Methuselah pulling off his outer robe. When had the old man arrived?

"Pull him back a bit." He pointed.

Zarah and Salbeth grabbed Shem under his arms and dragged him away from the fire.

Shem cried out in pain as the movement jolted his injured shoulder.

"Go." Methuselah jerked his head toward the burning ship and pressed his robe against Shem's wound. "He will be fine."

The women turned back to the crisis.

Zarah allowed herself only a glance at the ship before running forward to continue stomping out the grain fire. But the glance gave her hope that perhaps they were winning the battle. The flames seemed a bit less intense. The burning section of the ship more confined.

Noah seemed more confident as well. She sensed him moving closer in to the flames.

But perhaps it was too soon.

"Father!" Japheth's voice carried above the sound of Ham's mallet. "Your tunic!"

Zarah followed Japheth's voice to the hem of Noah's garment, which had caught fire.

Noah swatted at the flame as though it was of no consequence, given the larger crisis. But the loosely woven cloth ignited quickly. The lower half of his left side was suddenly aflame.

Zarah and Japheth reached him simultaneously. Japheth barreled over his father, knocking him to the ground. He covered Noah's body with his own.

Zarah snatched up a charred blanket that had been tossed aside and joined Japheth to smother the burning tunic.

"Enough, enough! I am not on fire, the ship is!" Noah pushed them both away, started to stand, and then fell back.

"Noah, your leg!" Zarah knelt at his side, put a hand on his knee to still him, and examined his thigh where his tunic had burned away. An angry burn blistered there, and the hair of his leg had been singed away entirely.

Noah put a hand to his thigh, as if to cover himself, then winced and pulled it away. He still lay on the ground, propped on his elbow.

Zarah ripped a clean section from the blanket and wrapped his leg with it. He barely noticed her actions, his eyes on the ship.

"There, Ham." He pointed. "Just there. Yes. That's the last of it now." He sank back onto the ground, eyes closed, as Zarah finished tending his leg.

"Shem?" He opened one eye and turned his head toward their son.

Methuselah held up a hand from where he leaned over Shem. "A cut in the fleshy part of his shoulder. Not deep. It will heal."

Zarah exhaled in relief and gripped Noah's hand.

He returned the pressure but turned back to the ship.

The others continued to stomp out any smoldering grain they spotted, until finally it seemed that every flame had been extinguished.

And then they were all on the ground. Panting, sweating, but the rest of them unhurt. And the ship was saved, if not whole.

The smell of burning bitumen still hung heavy in the afternoon air as they surveyed the damage.

Zarah took in each of the family members. "Where is Salbeth?" Her voice was tinged with fear.

Shem shot up to a sitting position with a yell of pain.

Methuselah pushed him back down. "She is right there, coming back."

Indeed, Salbeth was already on her way back to them, carrying two large wineskins in her hands. The girl always seemed to anticipate what was needed, ready before anyone else thought to move.

She stepped now, from one to the next, carrying the wineskins to each so they could at least partially slake their thirst.

Zarah gave her a grateful smile and a pat on the hand when Salbeth reached her.

They sat in silence for some time, staring up at the ship, each with their own thoughts and none willing to share, it seemed.

The ground around the base of the ship was littered with blackened boards, still smoking in the afternoon sun. The hull of the ship now had a gaping hole, higher than any of their heads, and perhaps a dozen cubits wide. Big enough to walk four teams of yoked oxen through, with room left for the farmer and his family.

Finally, beside her, Noah spoke.

"The torch is still there, no doubt. Under the rubble."

His voice was low and quiet, but it carried across what seemed like an unnatural stillness since the fire had been put out.

Zarah frowned. "What torch?"

Ham sat with his knees drawn up, his arms draped over them. "When we arrived, after we spotted the fire, there was a burning torch on the ground." He pointed to the blackened hole. "There. It had been left at the base."

Zarah sucked in a breath. "Someone deliberately—"

"What else could it be?" Ham's voice betrayed the anger they all felt. "The ship would not suddenly start burning of its own accord."

Shem growled. "We will find this person, and—"

"And what, Shem?" Noah sighed. "And what? What good would it do?"

"Perhaps none, Father. But someone must be made to pay for this damage!"

Noah shook his head. "We do not have time for revenge."

"I speak of justice!" Shem was sitting again now, despite Methuselah's clucking disapproval.

Noah ground the heels of his hands into his eyes. "Sadly, I believe all we have left is justice. But the justice to be meted out will not be at our hands."

Ham huffed in exasperation. "I am so tired of your insistence that the end of all things is coming, Father." He waved an arm at the ship. "Can you not see that this is foolishness? When will we return to farming? Grow our income, so we can buy the things we need? The rest of the city buys and sells and indulges itself in luxuries. Why must we be different?"

Noah said nothing, and Zarah could feel his silence in her own heart. Her sons would think that his silence was disapproval. But she knew it was a deep and heavy sadness. The sadness he always carried, for the dark and lost world around them.

Japheth, sitting near his brother Ham, reached out to punch his shoulder lightly. "What do you need with luxuries, Ham? You are spoilt enough."

His jest fell heavily. No one was ready for lighter spirits yet.

"So," Noah said, looking up at the ship. "We have a large repair to make." He glanced at Shem. "We have injuries to tend. And"—he lowered his head—"it appears we have an enemy working against us."

"Is that all, Father?" Ham's voice was tinged with sarcasm. "Let's not forget that we have no money."

As if to punctuate the dire pronouncements, a strange, rumbling *boom* sounded around them, and the grain field trembled and shook beneath the huddled family.

CHAPTER EIGHT

Zarah crossed the field to the small house where Methuselah had lived all his life, where Lamech and even Noah had been born. She was glad he stayed close, even when Noah's siblings had moved to the center of Kish.

She found the old man sitting on his roof, watching the early-morning sun as it rose.

He turned to her as she reached the roof, eyebrows raised in question. He looked tired and worn.

"They are awake but not off to work yet."

He breathed deeply and returned his gaze to the sun. "Yesterday was a hard day."

She felt he spoke of more than the physical exertion of the day, but she chose to answer as if that were the only struggle. "Yes, even Noah has agreed that a few hours of extra rest this morning would be acceptable. His burn gives him pain."

"And Shem's shoulder?"

"Salbeth dressed it well, with a healing poultice of aloe leaf and sage, and some fresh cloths. It doesn't impede his movement much."

Zarah spread a mat on the roof and sat at his feet in her usual way. "And how do you fare this morning? I wish you would have stayed the night with us."

"Hmm. As I said last night, the One God and I had much to discuss. And none of you wants to hear my mutterings."

Methuselah often wandered the fields, talking to God, Zarah knew. She would watch him sometimes, wondering if he heard things as well as spoke them. Did the One God speak to him, as He had done just that once for Noah? But Methuselah had not been out walking last night, she guessed. Not after the way the earth itself had seemed angry.

"And what did you and your God work out between you?" She asked it with a smile, but he did not join her in it.

Methuselah shrugged and patted her head with his blue-veined hand. The gesture seemed to cause him pain. When had he grown so weak?

"It is not for us to always have answers."

She leaned her head against his leg. "Do we *ever* have answers, Grandfather? It seems today brings only questions."

"What questions trouble you?"

She sighed. "Is Noah right about the earth-shaking yesterday? Does it mean that the end is truly near? Who would have tried to burn the ship? Will Noah finish in time, especially now that he and Shem must heal? Where will we get the money for the supplies—"

Methuselah was laughing. "Yes, yes, I see you do indeed have questions. And yet I believe that there is more under all of those, farther back even. Yes?"

She half smiled and looked toward the rising sun. "It has been so hard. You know. You have lived many years, and you've seen what the world has become. What our lives have become."

"You find it difficult to remain apart? To keep yourself from the evils of the world?"

"Not difficult to renounce the ways of my neighbors." The moon god cult and its hold on her former life had made it easy. "Never that. But it is hard to see friends turn their backs when you walk past them on the street. To hear children mock your family. To have merchants refuse to sell us their goods because they believe we will bring the wrath of the moon god on the city."

"Yes, I have seen how hard all of that is on him."

Zarah bristled, drew away and looked up at Methuselah. "On *him*? On Noah, do you mean?"

He grinned. "I know it has been hard on you. But for Noah as well. And he has been doubly hurt to know that he does not have the support of even his wife and sons."

Zarah's legs felt stiff, sitting on the chill of the roof. She stood and crossed to the roof-wall, her back to Methuselah. "I don't know how you can say that." She jutted her chin toward the ship across the field. "Does that look like something that was built without support?"

"Your sons have swung a hammer, it is true. But they have never fully believed Noah's words. Never truly joined him. Nor have you."

She shrugged, her back still toward him. "What difference does that make?"

The silence behind her lengthened, until she finally turned to him. "Noah has his sons to help with the labor. And the boys have wives now, Grandfather. Each one of them younger and stronger than I, and just as competent to take care of the household. Noah has his project and his words from God. You are revered by all of them as Eighth and relied upon for wisdom." She breathed heavily. "So, I will say it again, what difference does anything that I do make now? I am not even able to successfully sell my jewelry to make money for supplies. Truly, I have become the least important member of this family."

And if you knew all of my past, you would find me the most distasteful as well.

"What do you think goes on in that heart of Noah's every day, my child?"

She blinked at the question that did not seem to follow any logic. "I—I think that he is focused on nothing more than building his ship."

"And why?"

"Because that is what he believes God told him to do."

"So he does it only out of blind obedience?"

She dropped her shoulders, which had grown tense. "No, I know that he wants to protect us from what is coming."

"As he has wanted to protect you all, every day of his life, yes?"

"Yes."

"And not you alone but the city too? The world?"

She nodded and looked away. How could she have criticized Noah? "He tried for so many years to turn people's hearts back to the One God."

"And now?"

"And now he knows he has failed. That they cannot be saved. That they will be destroyed."

"And so?"

"And so he is heartbroken."

The sun had lifted fully above the horizon now, but the world was still unnaturally silent, with no birdcalls, no bleating of far-off sheep or lowing of cattle.

"What does a heartbroken man need, my child? Does he need a stronger hammer?"

"No."

"Does he need more willing laborers?"

"No."

"More money?"

She grew silent, unwilling to answer further because of the condemnation of herself that it would lead to.

"What does a heartbroken man need?"

She sighed again. "He needs a wife. A wife who believes in him and supports him."

Methuselah smiled. "And the other things wouldn't hurt, either."

She laughed and sat again at his feet. "Tell me what the One God says to you, Grandfather. Why did He not tell Noah to take you on the ship? You are the best of all of us, to be sure."

"That is a secret, I'm afraid. Between me and the Creator. Perhaps I will tell you one day."

She did not contradict him. But if the earth-shaking was a sign, as Noah said it was, they did not have many days left for the sharing of secrets.

"I want to help him."

The words bubbled up from somewhere, and she realized that she had never before spoken them. Never before even felt them.

"That is good."

"What shall I do?"

"You will do what is right, child, I am certain of it. And Noah will see that your heart is for him. He will see."

Yes, she would do what was right. But what was the right thing to do? How could she best help with a project that required skills and strength she did not possess?

She looked up to the old man to ask more questions, but his eyes were closed.

"Have you eaten this morning, Grandfather? You seem so tired."

He smiled. "I would not say no if you wanted to fix me something."

She left him an hour later, dozing on his rooftop, his belly full of warm broth and bread. In the hour she had tended to him, the right thing had come to her. She doubted that Noah or her sons would agree.

But she did not intend to ask their permission.

CHAPTER NINE

Noah awoke disoriented. The light filtering through to the sleeping room he shared with Zarah was too bright to be morning. He rolled to one side, then moaned as his burned leg brushed the rough weave of his striped sleeping mat.

The memory of the day before slipped into place. Yes, it was nearly midday now, no doubt. He had risen with the dawn as usual, taken food with the family, and then declared that neither he nor Shem would work that morning and instead rest their injuries. He had inspected Shem's shoulder carefully this morning, guilt pressing against his chest. None of this would have happened if he had not demanded their help with the ark.

Ham and Japheth did their best to look concerned for the two men, rather than gleeful at the unexpected reprieve, and exited the morning meal quickly, before Noah had a chance to suggest that the two uninjured men work alone, which he now regretted.

Ah, well. They were so far behind now, what did one more morning matter? It seemed impossible that they would finish before the end. The earth-shaking that had happened yesterday after the fire had been only the latest in a series of signs that something terrible was soon to come. And now that their saving ark had a large gap burnt through one end, it seemed doubtful that they would survive it.

Noah shifted his position on the mat to relieve the pain in his leg but did not yet rise.

Every time these doubts assailed him, he did the only thing he knew to do. He prayed.

God of my fathers, of Adam and Seth, of Enosh and Kenan, Mahalalel and Jared, God of all my fathers who have gone to earth, and God of Enoch who walks still with You, and of my father Lamech. Blessed be Your Name. You need only speak Your will to me, and I will obey.

And then he listened. Listened with eyes closed, hoping against hope that the Voice would come again. The Voice he had heard once so clearly and now sometimes doubted.

How do we finish? Will You hold back the waters, even if we continue to fail You? Will You save us, even still?

There was no answer.

And so he pulled himself to sitting, and then to standing. Because the work must continue.

He dressed carefully, binding his burn with fresh cloths, and ascended the steps to the roof, where he could smell the midday meal being served.

The family was there, without Zarah.

Noah raised his eyebrows, searching the roof.

"She went to Grandfather," Salbeth answered his unspoken question.

He growled in frustration. They still must go to Barsal and demand payment, and he had promised her that he would not go without her. She feared for his safety, that he understood. But it grated on him that he had made the promise.

He had another task for this afternoon anyway, so let Zarah fritter away the hours at the feet of his grandfather if she wished.

Lying on his sleeping mat, he had not heard the Voice, but he did get an idea. The destruction caused by the fire was significant. They needed help, especially with Shem's injury and his own slowing them down. He would go to the only people in the city who might possibly be willing to help them make the repair.

He would ask his brothers.

When the meal was cleared and Zarah still had not returned, Noah set out for the city once again, this time alone. He walked slowly, favoring his injured leg and angry that he was forced to do so.

His two brothers, Eber and Reu, lived in the heart of the city, in a single home with their two wives. Noah's two sisters had already gone to earth, both in childbirth. He had feared such an outcome with each of his sons' births, but thankfully Zarah had been strong. Strangely, none of his sons' wives had yet borne a child. It had been a source of pain for all three, and Noah dreaded the day that one became with child if the other two remained barren.

But perhaps it was the grace of the One God, who knew what was to come, that kept their wombs from being fruitful. At least for now.

Eber and Reu, on the other hand, had too many sons and daughters between them for Noah to count. And he knew little of them, since his brothers had long ago begun to treat him as an outsider.

Why would today be any different? But he was desperate.

The street was quiet today. No doubt the ground tremors yesterday had everyone concerned and staying indoors.

Unless they are all at the moon god's temple, prostrating themselves and pleading for mercy.

The grudging frustration bloomed in his chest. Why were they always willing to bow the knee and beg the moon god, but the true One God who had provided them sunshine and crops and children all their lives went ignored or even scorned?

Eber's wife, Pisha, was outside the house, dumping a pot of refuse into the street. She looked up at Noah's approach, scowled in recognition, and ducked under the doorway without a word.

Noah followed her in, not waiting to be invited.

"Eber."

His brother was sitting on the floor, working on a tool he probably used for tanning the hides that brought his income. He scrambled to his feet, anger in his eyes.

"What are you doing here, Noah? You cannot be here!"

Noah glanced at Pisha, still scowling.

Eber's outburst brought Reu and his wife from a back room.

So, everyone was at home today.

"I need your help, Eber. And yours, Reu." He bowed to his younger brother in the doorway.

Reu folded his arms over his chest. "What kind of help?"

"The ark—" He nearly choked on the words when he saw the expression in the eyes of them all. "There was a fire yesterday, and the ark was damaged—"

Eber laughed. "Do you think the whole city does not know of your ship, of your fire, of your lunacy?" He pointed to the front door. "You need to leave before someone sees you. It has taken us years to wash the stink of your madness from our family so that those in the city will buy and sell with us. We want nothing to do with you."

"We cannot finish it alone. I can pay you." But even as he spoke the words he had practiced on his walk into the city, he knew how futile they were. Eber and Reu wished he did not even live. They would never help with the building of the ark. Noah had prayed to God on his way that his brothers would agree and that their change of heart would be enough to secure them and their families a place on the ark when the end came.

But that was not to be. God had been silent, but his brothers had spoken. And they had spoken hatred.

Reu pushed into the front room, advancing on Noah and forcing him backward to the door. "There is nothing you could pay us that would convince us to put our families in danger."

"Danger?" Noah braced a hand against the doorframe before Reu pushed him into the street.

Reu laughed in scorn. "Did you think your fire fell from heaven?"

"What do you know of it?"

"More than you, it would seem."

Noah glanced at Eber, but he said nothing.

Pisha, however, had never been one to keep her mouth closed when there was news for the telling. "The whole city knows that you are to be considered an enemy of Sin."

Well, that is true enough.

"I make no secret of the fact that I serve the One God, and no false god such as Tikov has erected."

Pisha clucked her tongue. "And it's talk such as that which has caused you to fall out of favor. Are you then surprised that someone has tried to burn your ridiculous boat? That your brothers would rather go hungry than take your money?" She wiped her hands on the cloth she had been holding, then snapped it out at him, catching him on the hand with a stinging edge. "Go on. Go home to your mad family."

"Brothers, I beg you—"

"We will not build your ship!" Eber was pushing him out now as well.

"Not the ship—I beg you to repent! To turn back to the One God—"

"Enough!" Reu and Eber each put a hand on his chest, shoved him backward into the street, and slammed the door.

CHAPTER TEN

Zarah crossed the fields from Methuselah's house while the morning sun was still burning off the mists of dawn. She put the ship between her and her family home, glancing that way occasionally to ensure that none of them were watching a lone figure skirt the far side of their fields, taking the long path toward the edge of the city.

Noah had told her that he didn't wish for her to go alone to the market, nor to go to see Barsal. But he had not forbidden her to visit her former friend, Etana. At this hour, Barsal would be conducting business in the city and his wife would surely be at home. Zarah would plead with the woman to convince her husband to pay for the necklace he had taken.

She allowed herself a moment to imagine Noah's response when she poured the silver into his palm. It would be enough to purchase supplies to repair the fire damage, and even more besides. Perhaps enough even to finish the ship. She smiled to herself as she hurried along the dusty path. Her sons' wives could clean and cook and mend, but none of them had a skill that brought money to the family. Zarah was still useful, still worth something to the family project.

The family project.

Something had shifted within her, there at Methuselah's feet. Some seed of belief had sprouted. If not belief in Noah's God, at least belief in Noah himself. Her husband had been good to her all the years of their marriage. There was no reason to think he had become a different man, even if his shipbuilding had consumed his attention for these past few years.

And so, she would do whatever she could. Whatever would help him finish. If the end of all things did come, they would be ready. And if it did not come, if Noah was as mad as the people of the city claimed, at least the ship would be complete and they could all go back to farming.

A fox rustled out of the dry grass at the side of the road and scuttled across her path. She slowed to let it cross and lifted her eyes to the street that began ahead. She would take the main street through the city, to the other side where Etana's home sprawled in the midst of a vast vineyard.

She kept her head down as she passed through the city. It was early yet, and there were only a few people about, mostly women headed to the central well to draw water. A few children playing in the street.

She quickened her pace as she passed the home of Noah's two brothers and their wives. She would not be welcome there for a visit and had no desire to encounter any of them, especially not Eber's wife, Pisha, who had become bitter and cruel as she aged and had no use for Noah or any of his family.

Soon enough she had Etana's home in her sight. It stood wider than nearly any home in the area of Kish, with rooms enough for all of Etana's children and their families. Each of Barsal's sons worked the vineyard with him, and the wine they created traveled all the way to Tikov, perhaps beyond. The wine had made them rich.

And greedy.

It incensed her that Barsal would refuse to pay for her jewelry when he could so obviously afford it.

What had Etana thought of the necklace? Would she be delighted with Zarah's handiwork, and appalled that Barsal had cheated Zarah to obtain it?

She imagined the necklace around Etana's throat, its delicate gold filigree glinting in the morning sunlight. A memory came flashing into her heart, of Etana, years earlier, bent over the birthing stool while still wearing another fine necklace of red rubies her husband had given her.

It had been a hard labor, long and more painful than most. Zarah remained by her friend's side in the large back room of the house, despite the protests of the midwife, who did not appreciate Zarah's suggestions or her presence. But when the midwife tried to push her from the room, Etana had gripped Zarah's hand and pleaded with her eyes that Zarah stay.

Zarah returned the grip, then winced as another contraction hit Etana and she countered it by nearly crushing Zarah's hand. She knelt beside the birthing stool, whispered encouragement to Etana, pushed the sweaty strands of hair from her forehead.

Etana was a few years younger, and this was her first child. Zarah already had three young sons at home. The midwife might be the expert, but there was no substitute for a friend who understood.

"Yes, Etana, that is good. You are doing so well." She kept up the steady flow of encouragement as the contraction subsided.

Etana relaxed a bit, leaned her head on Zarah's shoulder. "I cannot do it."

"Of course you can. You are so strong."

The labor went long into the night. Zarah asked Barsal to send word to Noah that she was safe and would not leave her friend. She kept Etana's forehead cool with cloths dipped in a nearby water jug and kept the room just warm enough, but not too warm, with the dung chips fed to a small brazier in the corner.

And in the morning, just as the sun was edging over the horizon, the cries of a newborn boy were their reward.

The midwife had finally accepted her presence and even handed baby Dzumid to Zarah first, to let her put the squalling bundle into Etana's weary arms.

Even now, the memory of nestling the tiny Dzumid against Etana's chest, with her red-ruby necklace still intact, made Zarah smile.

But it had been many years ago. Today, it was an aging male servant who greeted Zarah at the doorway to Etana's home and asked her business there.

"I am—a friend. Zarah. Come to visit Etana."

The bony man looked her over with a disdainful eye. Did he know who she was? He disappeared into the home.

A moment later Etana was at the doorway, eyes wide. She grabbed Zarah's wrist and pulled her into the house, her head swiveling to scan beyond Zarah as if looking for someone.

"What are you doing here? Did anyone see you come?"

Zarah looked behind her, toward the city. "I—I don't think so."

Her friend was unchanged, though Zarah hadn't seen her in years. Still plump with good health, still with the little crinkles at the corners of her eyes that evidenced her frequent smile.

But she was not smiling today.

Etana backed away and put her hands to her hips, as though scolding young Dzumid. "What do you want, Zarah? Why have you come?"

Zarah squared her shoulders and tried to still the pounding of her heart. Their friendship had been lost years ago, but still she had not expected anger.

"Can we go inside?" Zarah looked over Etana's shoulder, toward the central courtyard of the house, which was still the largest Zarah had ever seen.

Etana huffed, glanced through the open doorway once more, then spun and led the way deeper into the house.

The garden in their courtyard boasted aloe and cress, and the pungent smells of mint and sage wafted across Zarah and caused a pang of hunger.

Etana extended a hand to a white alabaster bench, still unsmiling.

Zarah crossed the courtyard and lowered herself to the bench. Her fingers gripped its smooth surface. Beside the bench, a tiny pool boasted several bright orange fish that swam in circles, unconcerned with the emotions above them.

Etana stood opposite her, arms folded over her ample chest.

"How do you fare, Etana? Is your family well? The children must be well-grown by now—"

Etana shook her head. "I will not speak to you of my family. I allowed you into my home because of our former friendship. But you must state your business, and then you must leave."

A cool breeze filtered through the courtyard, and Zarah tried to let it calm her heart.

"Etana, you speak of our former friendship, but I love you still. I never wanted us to grow apart, even if our husbands cannot—"

"Do not speak of my husband! Or even of yours!"

Zarah stood, crossed to where Etana faced her, and grabbed the woman's hands. "Etana, please. Think of what was once between us. What did I do to cause you to hate me?" She tried to force the tears back, but they spilled down anyway. "All I want is for us to be at peace. Can't we have peace?"

Etana closed her own eyes and sighed. Her shoulders fell as though she were exhausted. "I wish things were different, Zarah. I truly do. You were a good friend to me." Her eyes snapped open, and she pulled her hands from Zarah's grasp. "But that cannot be. Not now, when you and your family are trying to destroy everything that the god Sin blesses us with."

Zarah took a step back. "We have destroyed nothing! Noah wishes only to save—"

"Look here." Etana pointed to a small niche carved in the wall of the courtyard. "Do you see what has come of my household god?"

Two chunks of sculpture lay in the niche. Zarah moved closer to examine them.

It had been a statue of the moon god Sin. The upper half of the old man's body, with its flowing beard and cylindrical headpiece with a crescent moon atop, lay broken apart from the lower half of his seated figure. The god's eyes glittered, black chips of obsidian that seemed to accuse.

She turned back to Etana, the unspoken question in her eyes. How could Etana hold her responsible for this broken statue?

"Yes, you!" Etana nodded furiously. "In the earth-shaking that happened yesterday! Sin is angry at the way your family condemns him, and all who follow him. He shook the whole earth to show his displeasure!"

"Etana, do you not remember the ways of your childhood? When men still called only upon the name of the One God—"

"No!" Etana put her hands to her ears, as if she were a child throwing an angry fit at words from a parent she did not want to hear. Her eyes darkened and she shook her head, not in protest but as if something buzzed inside her mind that she could not be rid of. "Zarah, you must leave!"

This had been a fool's journey. Zarah hadn't even gotten the chance to ask Etana for the money, and clearly the woman had no interest in paying her. She didn't even wear the necklace Barsal had stolen. Perhaps she recognized Zarah's handiwork and refused to even accept it.

She wiped at the tears that still flowed and nodded. "I will go."

But when she turned toward the doorway, it darkened with the figure of a large man.

Barsal.

His bushy brows drew together as he took in Zarah beside the little shrine and Etana still covering her ears. "What is going on here?"

CHAPTER ELEVEN

The slammed door of his brothers' house might as well have been a slap across Noah's face.

He stumbled backward from their shove, lost his footing, fell into the dirty street, and sat there stunned.

How had they come to this place?

They had grown up in the same house, the house where their grandfather Methuselah still lived. Chased one another in the fields together, then worked in the fields side by side. They had taken wives around the same time, had children that played together.

And yet somewhere, their paths had diverged. The call of the Other Way was strong on his brothers, and they did not resist. Despite the teaching and even the pleading of the fathers before them, Eber and Reu had made their decision and turned their back on the One God.

And turned their back on Noah.

He climbed to his feet slowly, brushed the dirt from his tunic, then his hands. There was shame in being knocked to the ground by one's own brothers, to be sure. But the anger he would have expected to feel did not come. The end was too close now. He could feel it and smell it, and he knew what it meant for Eber and Reu and their wives. How could he be angry, when they had chosen death?

He stared at the closed door for a few more moments. What could he say to change their minds? How could he convince them that they were destined for destruction?

You cannot.

He heard the two words only in his mind, but they seemed to come from outside of himself. Whispered to him by the One God, perhaps. Words to reassure him that he had done all he could. He turned finally from the door and trudged toward home.

So, there would be no help from his brothers. And it would seem that the entire city had turned against them, so even if he could convince Barsal to pay the money he owed, there would be no one to hire. They were on their own.

All that was left was faith that God would hold back the end of all things until Noah finished the ark. But was it not arrogant to think that God would change His mighty plans, simply to accommodate Noah's lack of skill and money?

He became aware slowly that he was being followed. A giggling and shuffling sound behind him alerted him that he had a small retinue of children at his back. He slowed and turned to them, fists on his hips.

They drew back as a group, as if frightened of the crazy old man. There were seven or eight of them, all boys.

"What do you want?" He kept his voice at a growl, not feeling the patience for children today.

But his threatening tone seemed to embolden rather than frighten them.

One of them, clearly the leader of the pack, stepped forward, holding something behind his back. He grinned a gap-toothed smile, then jerked his hand from behind him and flung an earthen cup full of water at Noah's face.

"There is your flood, old Noah!"

The boys howled with laughter.

"You had better run to your ship before you drown!"

"No, he can't!" Another boy piped up, pointing beyond Noah toward the field at the edge of the city. "His ship has a big hole in it!"

"My father says that the moon god Sin shone down so brightly in the night that he burned a hole in the side of Noah's ship, to teach him a lesson."

Another boy skipped forward from the back of the group and hurled something else.

Not water this time. A rock. It skimmed Noah's cheek as it sailed past.

Noah felt his cheek, but it was only a scratch. "Go home!" he yelled. "Home to your evil houses and your evil parents!"

But they only laughed and began to scoop up pebbles from the street and fling them at him.

And just as with his brothers, his anger drained away and was replaced by such a deep sadness he could hardly bear the weight of it.

Them too, God? All of them? Even the children?

For as cruel as they were, they were only repeating the words they'd heard at home.

"Stop." He held up his hands. "You must listen."

But they thought he feared their little pebbles, and they only advanced on him with more.

He grabbed the two nearest him, clutched them to himself. Felt himself weeping. "Please, please, you must listen!"

The two boys screamed at finding themselves in his grasp, and twisted from him, kicking at his shins and yelling.

Adults were taking notice now, emerging from homes to see what the noise was about.

"What are you doing with those boys?" A yell from within a doorway.

Noah released his hold on them, swiped at his tear-streaked face. He could feel the mud there, his tears mixed with the dirt the boys had rained on him.

He stood there in the center of the street, with the gang of boys in front of him, their parents and neighbors ranged in a half circle behind them and felt the hatred of every person in the street flow toward him.

He turned and ran.

He did not run because he feared them. He ran because he could not bear to look at them and see their future.

Head down, he barreled toward his fields and house and ark, forcing himself to focus on the pain in his leg as he ran and the plan for repairing the ark, and anything at all besides the faces of those children who understood nothing of what was to come.

Finally, finally when his lungs burned and chest heaved and his leg could no longer manage the pain, he slowed and lifted his eyes toward the edge of the city and his field.

And drew up short at the sight.

Smoke rose in the air above the ark. Black and plumy, unlike anything he'd seen before.

No, no, no. They could never recover from another fire.

Despite his pained leg, he took to running again. But the closer he got to the ark, the more confused he grew. The black smoke did not seem to get closer. It came from behind the ark, and at first he thought it was the far side burning. But no, now that he was nearly across the field, he could see that the smoke was farther on, beyond the ark.

He reached the side of the hull, ran through the doorway and up the two sets of ramps to reach the roof, still unfinished.

His sons and their wives already stood on the roof, their eyes on the sky beyond the ark.

"What is it? What is burning?" He grabbed the side beam with both hands, breathing heavily.

"The mountain." Shem's words were clipped, fearful.

Noah lifted his eyes and squinted into the distance, to the line of mountains that had stood at his horizon since childhood. He traced the jagged line of their summits, like the scales of a fish bent forward as it leaped into water, familiar to him for all the years of his life.

But there, in the center of the horizon, one of the fish's scales was missing, a plume of black smoke in its place, as though the mountain itself had been thrown upward, burning, into the sky.

Indeed, it appeared that the mountain was burning.

Would the wind shift, and bring the black smoke this way?

"Surely if they see this, they will believe." He spoke the words to himself, but the others heard.

"Believe what, Father?" Shem's voice was full of challenge. "You have been telling us for years, been telling *everyone* for years, that you must build a ship because the world will be destroyed by water. And yet all we have is the earth rumbling beneath our feet and the mountains burning over our heads."

"But it must be a sign—"

Ham waved a hand in disgust. "If these are signs, we would be better off to dig a hole and shelter ourselves." He inclined his head toward the end of the boat where the fire had eaten away the wood. "We are more likely to be burned than drowned."

"Where is your mother?"

He needed her by his side right now. After the taunts of both his brothers and the children in the streets, he could not also stand up against the derision of his sons.

Na'el huffed. "She still has not returned from the grandfather's house. Left us all day with the chores and expects us to prepare the evening meal as well."

Noah turned away from the boat's rail and left the younger part of his family behind. Perhaps it would be better, as Zarah must have felt, to spend time with those whose hearts were more fully committed. Not only to the One God, but to the ark He had commanded them to build.

CHAPTER TWELVE

Zarah's heart plummeted at the sight of Barsal in the doorway. She had counted on him being occupied in his vineyards during her visit.

"I don't know." Etana spread her hands. "She arrived only a few minutes ago. I told her to leave."

There was a note of nervousness in her former friend's voice. No matter how many jewels her husband gave her, Barsal was a hard man to please, to be sure.

Barsal turned his piercing glare on Zarah. "It seems you have been asked to leave. I suggest you do so, before you give me a reason to put you out myself."

"I did not come to make trouble, Barsal." Zarah moved away from the shrine. There was no reason to remind him of the suspicion that her family had caused their little false god to break into pieces. "I only came to talk to Etana, about the jewel—"

Barsal took a threatening step forward. "We have nothing to say to you and nothing to hear from you!"

"Please, Barsal, we need that money."

His cruel face twisted into mocking laughter. "Yes, I heard about your latest disaster. It is a good thing your ship sits in a field, for I do not think it would be much good at floating."

"What do you know of it?" She tried to keep the suspicion out of her voice. No need to anger him further by sounding as though she was accusing him.

He laughed again. "The whole city knows of it, Zarah. That the moon god burned a hole in the side of your husband's foolishness."

"Not unless the moon god leaves behind a burning torch."

Barsal shrugged. "Who can say?"

The words were casual but there was a knowing glint in his eye.

"So you know that we have need of new supplies, and right now, you are the only person in this city who owes us money."

Etana stood at the edge of the garden square, watching the conversation back and forth from Barsal's doorway to where Zarah stood, fingers twisting at her waist, beside the little pool of fish. "What money? What is she talking about, Barsal?"

"It is nothing." He advanced on Zarah. "Time for you to leave."

Desperation emboldened her. "Etana, did your husband not tell you that it was I who made the necklace of rubies in silver for you? I met him two days ago to sell it to him, but he refused to pay."

Barsal was upon her now, his hand gripping her wrist painfully.

But Etana wedged herself between them and pushed Barsal backward. "What necklace?" She swatted at his chest. "What necklace, Barsal?"

He held up his hands to ward off her blows. "I—I was going to give it to you as a surprise—"

"Then go and get it. Now." She smacked his chest again.

Barsal winced but did not move.

"That's what I thought! You've already given it, haven't you? But not to me!"

"Etana—"

"No!" She was shoving him backward now, and he nearly lost his footing on the lip of the stone path that bordered the garden. "If I see this piece on the neck of Belessa, I will rip it off and force it down that girl's throat, do you hear me?"

Zarah wanted no part of this argument that should be had in private. "Please, both of you, I don't want trouble. I just want you to pay me what's owed."

Etana spun on her, anger flashing in her eyes. "No one is going to pay you, Zarah! Don't you understand? Everyone in this city knows that you are to be cut off! No help. No money. No food. Nothing."

Zarah clutched her robe tighter around her chest. "Who? Who has given this instruction?"

Barsal was laughing again. "You ask this question? You, of all the people in the city, should know the answer!"

Etana turned her wrath back on her husband. "Do not try to make this about Zarah, you lying mongrel! Where is she? Where is that girl, and where is that necklace? You cannot expect me to be satisfied with nothing. If I must share you with her, the least you can do is bring the jewels to *me*!"

Zarah took advantage of their momentary distraction to slip around the two of them and move toward the door. What did Barsal's words mean? Who would have instructed the entire city to cut off her husband and his family? There was only one person she could think of with that kind of power, and he was more than a day's journey away. But Barsal's hints in the street a few days ago, and now his mockery—they both indicated that he knew more than he should.

"Where do you think you're going?" Barsal stepped away from his wife and grabbed her wrist again.

"I am leaving! As you asked." She tried to twist her hand from his, but his fingers were like iron bands around her wrist.

"Leave us, Etana."

Zarah looked to her one-time friend, pleading in her glance, and remembered again the night Etana begged her to stay by her in childbirth.

But Etana's face was set as stone-hard as her little moon god statue, and her dark eyes were just as cold. She whirled away, obviously still angry with her husband, but with no intention to come to Zarah's defense.

And then they were alone.

At least whatever Barsal had to say about her past would be said only between them.

He twisted her arm up behind her back and pulled her backward against his chest, to whisper in her ear.

"I hear you were a beautiful woman once, Zarah. The years have not been kind to you."

She laughed to herself, despite the pain in her wrist. If he meant to hurt her with his words, he would have to do better than insults about her fading beauty.

"I suppose that is why the temple had no further use for you, eh? Once your looks had passed, what purpose was there for you?"

"You have heard false rumors, Barsal." She tried to pull away from his hot breath against her neck. "I was never beautiful."

"Ah, then it seems you were *never* worth anything at all."

"The money, Barsal. Pay me and let me leave."

"You are stubborn, I will give you that." He pushed against her, forcing her into a march toward the doorway, her arm still twisted behind her back. Her wrist was beginning to throb.

He paused in the doorway, holding her away from him slightly to face the city ahead of them. Beyond it somewhere lay her fields, her house. Her ship. She lifted her eyes to draw strength from the knowledge that all of that waited for her, as soon as she got free of this dreadful man.

In the distance, against the late morning sun, a strange column of black seemed to drift upward from the horizon. Her stomach clenched. More fire?

But before she had time to figure it out, Barsal was shoving her outward, out of the doorway.

She fell forward.

He released her wrist just in time for her to catch herself as she fell. She cried out as the aching wrist took the weight of her body and crumpled under her.

Forehead in the dirt, she sucked in a deep breath and then pulled herself to standing.

Behind her, the door was already closed.

CHAPTER THIRTEEN

The heat of the sun kept Zarah's head bowed as she made her way home. Her hands were scraped from Barsal's shove from his doorway, and her wrist throbbed painfully. She rubbed at it with her other hand. Hopefully the swelling would not keep her from working.

Some noisy, grubby children played in the street near Noah's brothers' house, but she didn't slow to see if they were grandchildren to Eber or Reu. Her mind was on the altercation with Barsal, and the betrayal of Etana. Truly, there was no one left in this city, or in this world, who had a kind word for her or her family.

Never mind them. She still had ideas about how she could help her family. As long as Noah's overprotective spirit didn't get in her way.

She was halfway home before she remembered the glimpse of strange black smoke she'd seen from the doorway before Barsal threw her out.

It was still there, rising beyond the edge of the city. It didn't seem to be the ship. Not this time. She quickened her steps but half wished she could run the other way. Whatever lay ahead, she felt much too tired to face it.

As she crossed the final field before her home, she was certain now that the odd smoke had nothing to do with the ship.

At the base of the ship, Noah, his sons, and the wives were emerging into the sunlight.

She waved a hand, and caught the attention of one of the women, Salbeth most likely.

She caught up to them before they reached the house.

Noah was giving instructions to the other men, about the work they would do that afternoon.

Na'el looked Zarah over with a frown. "What happened? You are filthy."

Zarah brushed at the front of her tunic, stained with dirt where she'd fallen.

"I thought you were with Grandfather," Noah said, looking over her shoulder toward the city. "Where have you been?"

Zarah took a deep breath but did not answer. She was too tired to explain her morning to everyone. Perhaps if they were alone.

The men disappeared behind the house, probably for tools, but the three women and Noah remained.

"It doesn't matter where she's been, she has not been here." Na'el looked to Salbeth and Aris for support. "She thinks because we are younger that we should be made to do all the work, while she does whatever she wishes."

Zarah's fists clenched at her sides. "You ungrateful child! I have never spent a day in my life doing as I wish."

Na'el's eyes widened at the unexpected outburst.

Zarah sighed and shook her head, feeling remorse already. "I am sorry, Na'el. I spoke harshly. It has been a difficult day. Please forgive me."

But Na'el had already recovered and held her head up in indignation. "Well, I—"

"Hush, girl." Noah's words were for Na'el, but his eyes were on Zarah. "Get back to the house. Mother and I need to talk."

Na'el snorted and twirled back to the house, with Salbeth and Aris trailing behind.

Zarah pointed to the sky beyond the ship. "A far-off fire, so large that we see the smoke?"

He closed his eyes briefly. "It is the mountain itself. Burning up into the sky."

She creased her forehead in question, but Noah only shook his head.

"Come," he said. "Sit." He led the way to the bench they kept at the side of the house, near the patch of grapes that now languished from inattention.

His kindness brought tears again, but she also sensed that he was as tired as she and needed to sit in the cool of the shade, away from the tensions of the household.

"I have been to see my brothers," he said when they were seated alongside each other.

Strange that she had just passed that way today as well. She said nothing of this. Noah needed to speak.

"I had hoped to convince them to help with the repairs. For pay, even. Though I don't know where I thought to get the money. Still, I hoped that they would take pity or remember our former bonds, or…something."

"I take it they were not agreeable to your plan."

"Ha." The laugh was completely without humor. "They threw me out into the street."

Zarah brushed at the dirt on her knees.

"They believe that their ridiculous moon god burned a hole in our ship in the night."

She nodded. "I have heard that rumor."

"And they worry that any association with us, with *me*, will bring them to ruin." He pounded a fist into his thigh and looked away. "I cannot make them see that the opposite is true. They are headed for ruin now, and only turning back to the One God will save them."

"Noah, I went to Etana today."

He pulled away to glare across at her. "You what?"

"I thought perhaps if it was just the two of us women… We were once so close. I hoped she would see reason and pay the money that Barsal owed." She finished the explanation with a strangled half sob, waiting for Noah's anger.

But he turned to face ahead again, and then wrapped an arm around her shoulders.

"I take it she was not agreeable to your plan."

Zarah smiled and leaned her head against his shoulder. "They threw me out into the street."

Noah kissed the top of her head.

It was a small gesture, one he'd performed a thousand times in their years together, but it had been a long while and it brought fresh tears to her eyes.

"They also believe the silliness about Sin burning our boat. But they told me that the city believes yesterday's earth-shaking was also a result of the god's anger because of us."

"*Our* boat?"

She elbowed him lightly in the ribs. "Are you listening? They think we are at fault—"

"I am listening." He pulled her tighter. "So, they threw you out. Even your friend Etana could not be convinced to do the honorable thing."

"Well, it didn't help that apparently the necklace was not for her."

"What?" Noah looked into her face, then started laughing.

"How can you laugh? Barsal is an awful man!"

He threw back his head and laughed the harder. But a moment later he was wiping at his eyes.

The tears were not of mirth, Zarah knew. The day had hurt them both.

"Why must it be this way, Noah? Why couldn't the One God perform acts—like the earth-shaking—that would convince them all to return to Him? Why must they instead be destroyed?"

Noah was silent a moment, as though pondering her question.

"I met a man once," he said, "years ago, when there was still some lawfulness in the city and men who stole from others were punished for their crimes. This man had taken ten of his neighbor's sheep as his own and been caught. He was forced to pay a fine, but he didn't have it, and so he was locked away for a time, until his family could raise the money. I was a young boy, and my father took me to visit the man locked away. I'm not sure why."

Zarah watched Noah's eyes scan the horizon, as if searching for the memory.

"The thing I remember best about this man was his anger. He was being punished for his own wrongdoing, and yet there was no remorse. He was angry at everyone—at the neighbor whose sheep he stole, at the jailer, even at my father, who brought him food and spoke to him of the One God's love for him." Noah ran a hand over his beard. "I could not understand it. How he could be angry and not remorseful and feel only that he had been done wrong in being jailed?"

She waited, knowing the story would somehow answer her question.

"I think that is how it is with all of mankind now, Zarah. We have all done wrong. All of us. Me, my sons, even you." He squeezed her shoulder. "The whole world has stolen its neighbor's sheep and been asked to make restitution, but we have nothing with which to pay. And so we must suffer the consequences, and yet somehow there are so many who are angry at God and believe that they don't deserve His judgment."

He stood now and paced in front of her. "I have often wondered why God has chosen me, chosen our family. Because we are not without sin, either. But I think it is only this—that we have admitted our failing and gone to God for mercy. We do not shake our fists and insist that our condemnation is unde-served. And so, God grants us mercy." He looked out toward the city. "And for the rest of them, who still insist upon their own way...they have chosen their own reward."

With that he sank to the bench, head in his hands.

He wept for his brothers and their families, Zarah knew.

She wept for Etana and all the other friends of the past.

They sat there for quite some time as the sun sank lower in the afternoon sky, thinking on both the justice and the mercy of the God they served.

CHAPTER FOURTEEN

Noah left Zarah resting in their sleeping room and headed for the ark. After the morning she'd had, he hoped she would sleep away the remainder of the day's heat.

His own heart was not so restful, and he had other plans for the afternoon.

Though his wife feared for his safety and that of their sons, this latest insult from Barsal could not go unaddressed.

First he cheats my wife out of payment for her necklace, then he tosses her into the street like a beggar.

All three of his sons labored at various places within the ark, but it took him only moments to summon them to the entry planks and tell them of Zarah's confrontation with Barsal. He left off any explanation of his own similar encounter with his brothers. There was nothing to be gained by pushing in that direction. Barsal was another story. That money was still badly needed.

The three younger men were furious by the time he finished his tale. Even Japheth, typically so enthusiastically carefree, looked across the city toward Barsal's house and vineyard with a set jaw and piercing eyes.

Shem's anger was more vocal. "We should leave now." He pounded a fist against the side of the ark. "This injustice has gone on long enough, and only grows worse with waiting."

"I agree." Noah jutted his chin toward the inside of the ark. "But we should not go unarmed."

They were soon on their way across the field, each carrying a tool, recently used to create but now ready to destroy.

Ham's grip on his mallet was enough to turn his knuckles white. "Barsal's sons have been turning their faces from us for years now. They forget that we all once played in the same dirt."

Noah gripped Ham's shoulder. "We do not go to save our own reputation, Ham. We go for justice."

Ham shrugged away from his father's touch. "We each go for our own reasons, Father. Leave me to mine."

Noah sighed, a twinge of uncertainty bloomed in his belly. Was this confrontation ill-advised? Did they risk more than they would gain? But how else would they resupply to finish the ark?

They went first to Barsal's home, since his fields lay beyond the house, and because that was where Zarah had seen him last. An old servant answered the door but shook his head at their request.

"Who is there, Lugatum?" A female voice called from within the house.

Lugatum looked over his shoulder. "It is the woman's family, mistress. The one who came earlier."

Etana showed her face at the door, but it was not a welcoming face. Her glance took in the mallets and clubs they wielded, and her eyes widened. "What do you want?"

Shem spoke for the group. "Only what belongs to us. Nothing more."

"Barsal is not here. He is in the vineyard. With our *many* sons!"

Her implication was clear, but they were not about to be dissuaded now.

"Come," Noah said. "We will meet them in their fields."

Again, a flutter of concern bothered him. Again, he pushed it away. Not only pushed it away but forced himself to think instead of the ongoing insults to his wife. Used the thoughts to build up a righteous anger within him, enough to drive him forward.

One of Barsal's sons—Dzumid, if Noah remembered the boy's friendship with Japheth correctly—was the first to see them coming. From his place between the mounded rows of vines, he sounded a low whistle to his four brothers and father, who assembled a moment later. They stood with the solid gray sky at their backs, like six dark trees, broad and tall. They each wore the wine-red tunics they were known for, specially dyed by the grapes they grew.

Barsal spat on the ground at his feet. "What do you want, Shipbuilder?"

"You know what I want." Noah's grip tightened on his club.

"And you think to come and take it from me? Just like that? With only your three whelps to help you?"

The five sons emitted the same cackling sort of laughter and their silhouettes seemed to grow taller against the leaden backdrop of the sky. The rock-hard browned earth at Noah's feet made him feel hemmed in, trapped. He smelled the sweat of them all, the moisture in the air, and the sickly sweetness of overripe grapes.

His muscles were at war with his mind. He wanted to smash Barsal's mocking smile, wanted to take his sons and flee to safety, wanted to push Barsal into the same dirt he'd thrown Zarah into, wanted to leave this whole family to the coming destruction and having nothing more to do with them.

But the money. They must have the money.

Shem was not experiencing the same conflicted hesitation. He took a step forward, fire in his eyes. "You insulted our mother. More than once. You owe her money. And apologies." He raised his club with one hand and rested the knotted end of it in the other.

Several of Barsal's sons also took a step forward at Shem's advance.

"You'll get nothing here," one of them said. "Get back to your fire-burned insult to the gods."

It was the push Noah needed. He leaped forward, and felt his sons follow him into the fray.

Ten men in a brawl. Fists and clubs pummeled and jabbed. Sweat ran into Noah's eyes until they burned with salt. The wallop of clubs against backs and legs punctuated the grunts and heaves of the melee. The red of Barsal's family tunics mixed with flying drops of blood. The air grew thick, and Noah's chest felt airless, caving in.

What had he done?

A kick to his lower back drove him forward.

Brought his sons into a battle that was four men against six?

He caught himself as he fell to the dirt but lost his grip on his club.

Barsal's worthless and evil sons would be the death of his own righteous boys. The ark would go unfinished. The end would come and sweep away the women.

All these truths he saw in a flash.

A foot to his midsection drove the breath further from him, and black spots hung before his vision. In the sunless moment before he lost consciousness, he had only three more words.

God help us.

But then his vision was lightening, the world opened up again, and he saw that while the six larger men all stood and he and his sons were on the ground, it did not appear that Barsal would kill them after all.

"Go." Barsal's voice was thick with anger and hate. "You have your lives, only because of my son's soft heart."

Dzumid appeared to be holding back his brothers.

Noah slapped at the arm of Ham, who lay beside him. "Come. We are finished here."

The other three men lumbered to their feet, each holding their tongues, thankfully.

Noah wished for scathing words to deliver as they turned and limped away, but none came. They had once again been humiliated, for the sake of the ark the One God had instructed them to make. What was the sense of any of it?

His sons followed him wordlessly.

They were halfway home, moaning over their injuries, when a low whistle again sounded, this time behind them in the street.

Dzumid trotted toward them, holding a small pouch in his grip.

Japheth stepped forward, hands upraised. "No more, Dzumid. We are going home."

His former friend reached his side and stopped, breathing heavily. "Here"—he pressed the pouch into Japheth's hand—"but say nothing of this. And do not come to our fields again." With a last look at Japheth, he turned and ran back toward his home.

Japheth handed the pouch to Noah.

He untied the string slowly, his fingers stiff and swollen from the fight.

He poured the contents into Japheth's hand.

Seven small cubes of silver. More than enough to pay Barsal's debt.

Enough to purchase the rest of their needed supplies.

They stood staring at the silver, all of them. Noah breathed in a shaky breath and fought back tears. The pouring out of that silver was like warm water for washing, poured over his head—at once cleansing, soothing, and refreshing.

"Once again, my sons, the One God provides."

Ham opened his mouth as if to disagree or take credit, but Noah held up a hand. "No. No, we were unable to accomplish this. We took matters into our own hands and have only injury to show for it. This blessing is from the One God, who showed mercy on us despite our foolishness."

He closed his eyes and leaned his head back to the heavens. Later, later he would offer a sacrifice of praise and gratitude.

For now, he hoped that the One God could hear his thoughts, could hear his thanks.

While they wished to hurry home, each of them eager to have their wives tend their injuries, there were supplies to be purchased first. It was several hours before they finally returned, laden with a rented wagon full of lumber, sore muscles, and chastised but grateful hearts.

They were met at the door by Aris, whose look of worry seemed to be in place before she saw their injuries.

Noah's throat clenched. "What has happened?"

She pursed her lips. "I—I am not sure that anything has happened. It is just that—"

"Speak, woman!"

"Zarah has been gone again, for many hours. I looked for her at the grandfather's house, but she is not there. And—and her horse, Ibal, is also gone."

Noah tossed his mallet against the front wall of the house and ran his fingers through his sweaty hair. When, when, when would all of this end?

CHAPTER FIFTEEN

The journey to Tikov would take a day and a half.

If Zarah waited until first light to begin, she would still have to spend a night on the road. Better to leave immediately though the day was half gone, before the men returned from the afternoon's work on the ship and could prevent her.

It took only a few minutes to gather some bread and dried fish without the girls seeing and take it back to her sleeping room. She would wrap it all in one of the extra tunics from her basket, along with the rest of her clothes and an extra pair of shoes.

After removing the clothes from her deep basket, she reached to the bottom, to a tiny wrapped parcel lodged there and hidden from view. Without opening it, she secreted it in the folds of her extra tunics and slipped from the sleeping room and then the house.

The girls were probably on the roof or in their rooms, sleeping off the heat of the day.

She left the house and crossed quickly to the stable.

She laid a heavy blanket across Ibal's back, tied all her belongings, including the small pouch, into the largest of her robes, and slung it across his back before mounting. Her heart pounded, knowing she could be found out at any moment.

She directed Ibal out of the stable, across the fields, and down the road before even risking a look backward. The house lay undisturbed with the lowering sun behind it, its rays grazing the top of the ship beyond the house. She forced a calming breath. No one emerged looking for her, calling for her.

And no one would.

She used her heels to urge Ibal faster and put distance between herself and the family.

Would anyone care that she was gone? Would they admire her courage, going out to find a way to get what was needed, using her special skills? No, her husband would probably be angry at her foolishness. So be it.

At the thought of her skills, her hand went involuntarily to her sack of belongings, her fingers seeking out the little pouch she'd hidden there.

Seven jewels. Seven secret jewels, which represented their salvation.

Since all this business with the ship began and the community had begun to shun her family, each time she transacted business, selling off a new piece of jewelry, she kept back a little of the money. Noah never asked her exactly how high a price her piece had fetched, so she never needed to lie. She simply poured the tiny cubes of silver into his hands and didn't mention the extra she'd held back.

Over time, the extra had been enough to purchase a jewel not needed for the next piece. And then another. And another. Until she had seven stones—four carnelians, two lapis, and an onyx—that could mean the difference between life and death someday. When she had begun saving, she hadn't known when, or even if, that day would come. Only that she would do her part, whatever it might be.

And so she set her face toward Tikov, knowing she was the only one who could rescue them now. She hardened her resolve and pushed back the fear that had threatened to stop her since she left the house.

Hours later, in the growing darkness, the rocky sides of the path took on a menacing feel. Anyone could be hiding there. The smell of wet leaves and the taste in her mouth of the dried fish she'd chewed combined to make her feel like a stone lay in the pit of her stomach. She tried to keep her eyes on the road, an empty stare that did not give in to the fear of the dark shadows at the edges of her vision. But perhaps she should be more alert. Watching for robbers that lay waiting for stupid women to pass by unaccompanied in the dark.

Still watching the road, she felt again for the packet of jewels, but this time pushed it through the folds of cloth until it emerged and fell into her hand.

Better to keep it well-hidden. She worked it under her tunic, to the belt tied there, and secured it at her belly. The jewels were small and spread out in the pouch. They would likely not be noticed should anyone check.

She kept Ibal moving forward long past dusk, until she could barely see the road beneath his hooves, and she shivered in the cold. Finally, she slid from his back, pulled him into the shadows of the forest at the edge of the road, behind a particularly large boulder. She tied off his rope to a tree, put on every piece of clothing she'd brought except the extra sandals, and huddled beside the tree to wait for dawn.

The night passed in fitful starts and sudden jolts of fear. The sounds of animals, the squeaking limbs of trees, even the wind, seemed to conspire to keep her terrified and awake. She slept with arms hugging her middle, head against the rough bark of the tree. When the forest finally began to lighten around her, she climbed to her feet, body stiff and aching.

A sharp yell from the direction she'd come stilled her hands on Ibal's neck. She was still half-hidden behind the boulder, and in the dim light perhaps she'd go unnoticed. But who was yelling?

Three figures soon came into view, hurrying a donkey with a cart tied behind it.

Zarah squinted. A mother and two children? Yes, and perhaps another, smaller child in the cart.

And then a man, running up behind them, with some sort of club gripped in his hand.

Zarah sucked in a breath. The woman would have no chance against the man, and the children were too small to help.

She took a step forward, then hesitated. Slowed by thoughts of Noah and his need for supplies for his ship, and then of herself. The hesitation lasted only a moment. She must help if she could.

She left Ibal where he stood and stepped into the road.

The woman noticed her first, and a look of fear passed over her features as though Zarah were a threat rather than some-one who could help.

And then the man reached the woman and saw Zarah at the same moment.

Zarah moved toward the children, the oldest of which was a girl of perhaps six years and whose face betrayed terror.

Only a fraction of time passed, but something about the scene jolted Zarah's memory back to herself at six. Her father pushing her from behind, into the Temple of Tikov. Her palms had been slick with fear, her breathing shallow. She'd clutched at her father's tunic, only to have him pry her tight fingers from him and scold her sharply for acting like an infant.

Zarah lurched toward the little family, unthinking but determined to help.

But the man was embracing the woman. Urging the children to go faster. All of them glancing over their shoulders as though expecting someone to follow.

They were beside Zarah a moment later.

"Where is your husband?" the man asked, searching the forest beside the road.

Zarah said nothing. She traded glances with his wife, looked at the children.

"Are you alone?" The man jabbed his club back in the direction they had come. "Bandits on the road. I managed to outrun them, and they think I have nothing." He started to urge his little family forward again. "If they think we're worth following, they will be along soon."

His wife seemed reluctant to leave Zarah. "Are you alone?" She repeated her husband's unanswered question.

Zarah nodded.

"Join us, then, for as far as we travel the same direction. It's not safe."

Zarah hesitated only a moment. "Let me get my horse."

She didn't miss the look that passed between the couple. They had no horse, only a small donkey for their cart.

She grabbed her extra sandals and led Ibal from behind the boulder. She still wore all the clothes she had. "Once we are certain we aren't followed, we can have Ibal pull your cart. Perhaps we would make better time."

The husband gave her a grateful, if cautious, smile.

The little group moved forward, with frequent glances back down the road.

The journey to Tikov would still take the better part of the day, with many more opportunities for bandits to attack. But with this little family, perhaps she had a chance to at least reach Tikov.

Once inside its gates, however, she had to admit to herself that her mission was still a dangerous one.

CHAPTER SIXTEEN

Noah paced outside the house, too angry and frustrated to even have a conversation with the six inside.

Where had she gone? What impossible idea could have gotten into her head this time?

He could go after her, of course, but which direction? She would not have taken Ibal if she didn't intend to go far. To Tikov? But why?

And it grew near to nightfall. It would be foolish to try to track her down in the dying light, yet how could he leave her out there in the dark?

He crossed back to the front of the house and peered once more down the road that led away from Kish.

Bandits on the roads, women unexplainably disappearing. Not to mention the cold and wild animals. His heart pounded simply thinking about the possible dangers Zarah could encounter.

And it was yet another delay in their building efforts. Now, when they had finally been able to purchase supplies to finish the project. Now, when the earth rumbled and burned and clearly was near the day of the end.

He turned back toward the house, toward the ark, but knew that he must go after her. Must take his best guess as to her direction and start out. Despite the nearing of nightfall and the possibility that he would miss her on the road if she stopped to sleep in the shadows, if he waited for daylight, he would never catch up to her. It was an impossible situation.

He sighed and pushed open the door of the house. He would need some supplies. The inside of the house was warm and smelled of baking bread, making his mouth water and his heart ache that he could not rest his tired and beaten body near the fire.

"Father, she is treating us very unfairly!"

Na'el again, her sharp-featured chin jutting out in displeasure and her voice as shrill as the flute she loved to play.

He closed his eyes. Why must he deal with these women as if they were his children? Shouldn't their husbands be looking after them?

"Who has, Na'el?"

"Zarah, of course. Once again she has left us with all the work, as if we are her slaves."

Noah held up a tired hand. "Ham, see to your wife."

But Ham was just as angry. "How can she simply leave, knowing that—"

"Because she wants to help! She always wants to help!"

"Even so, Father," Shem said from the corner, "it seems irresponsible—"

"Enough! I need supplies. I will ride out to look for her. Pack some food. I will gather extra clothing."

"Do you want us to come?"

Japheth's voice was kinder, but it still grated on Noah. "No. Take the new supplies and work toward finishing before it's too late. I will go after your mother."

He crossed the room without looking at any of them. He was too tired to argue.

Inside his sleeping room, he gathered some extra tunics and a heavier blanket for warmth.

A rustle at the doorway turned him around. Salbeth stood hesitantly peering in.

"Yes?"

"I—I think I may know where she has gone."

He balled up the tunic and waited.

"Not long ago, I saw something in her basket while putting away clean clothes." Her glance flitted to Zarah's clothing basket.

He frowned. "What do you mean, you 'saw something'?"

"It was a pouch, and I—I was curious." She looked to the floor and grew silent.

"Say it then, girl. This is not a time for secrets."

"It was a pouch with jewels in it. Several of them, more than five, I think. She was hiding it there. She came in and found me looking at it and snatched it away."

"She tried to tell me about them, but I did not listen." Noah's patience was wearing thin, and he needed to start out. He crossed the room to Zarah's basket, lifted the thing, and dumped its contents in one motion. Only clothing fell to the floor. He tossed the basket to the ground.

"And why do you say you know where she has gone?"

"I think she has been hiding the jewels for a time when they were needed. She always wants to be…needed."

In this Zarah and Salbeth were much alike, and perhaps that was why the girl saw it.

"And?"

"And I know that Etana told her earlier that no one in Kish would trade any longer with our family, nor buy her jewelry. So I think she went to Tikov to sell the jewels."

Noah inhaled and looked around the room, as if more clues lay there. But she was gone, these jewels were gone, and Salbeth's explanation made good sense.

At least it gave him a direction in which to search.

It didn't take him long to pack up several large hunks of the freshly baked bread, still warm and crusty and topped with seeds, and to tie his belongings onto Hazir's back. He said his goodbyes and gave a few more instructions for his sons to work until the light was gone and then start again in the early morning if he had not yet returned.

"May the One God go with you and bring you back with our mother," Shem said as he turned the horse's head toward Tikov.

He nodded and smiled slightly at the sentiment, not trusting himself to respond without emotion to the reverent tone in Shem's voice.

And then he kicked Hazir into a gallop and went after his wife. The injuries to his leg from the fire, and the bruises he'd sustained at the hands of Barsal and his sons throbbed and burned and ached, but he forced himself to ignore them.

An hour later, there was still enough light to travel, but Hazir had long since needed a slower pace. Noah pushed him along, knowing that every minute that passed made it more difficult to find her, or perhaps made it more likely that she was in danger.

The passing minutes brought waves of worry, then anger, then even regret.

That his wife should be made to think she needed to provide a solution on her own meant that he had not made her feel protected and secure. The thought bit and scratched at him as he traveled.

He went as long and as far as he dared, until the darkness was thick enough to hide bandits waiting beside the road for lonely travelers, and the horse was getting nervous at every tree limb that cracked in the wind and every jackal that howled at an unseen moon. He huddled beside a tree and waited for light, dozing in small pieces of time through the long night.

As soon as the predawn light had filtered through the forest enough to see the road, he started out again, this time urging Hazir to speed along at his fastest pace. Hazir could outrun Ibal any day, and Noah doubted that Zarah had pushed her mount very hard. With the blessing of the One God, perhaps he could overtake her.

Sometime in the middle of the morning, he saw a misshapen lump of shadow far ahead on the road. He had been giving Hazir a break but now clucked to the beast to break into a run again.

Yes, the shadow ahead was definitely moving, but it looked too large to be a single woman on a horse. His heart thudded at double-speed. Had she already been surrounded by thugs?

He drew closer. Disappointment flooded him as he realized the shape was a small cart, with several people walking alongside. Not Zarah.

Perhaps they had seen her, however. He kicked at Hazir's sides and pushed forward.

There was a man, two or three children, and perhaps two women. And a donkey? Something else drew the cart, with the donkey walking beside. A strange group.

But then something about one of the women... He leaned forward over Hazir's head, squinting into the dim morning light.

Zarah.

He almost yelled but didn't want to frighten them all. Instead, he urged Hazir faster and sped toward the little group.

And then just before he would have called out to them, a knot of dark figures sprang from the woods at the edge of the road.

Robbers!

The call of greeting that had been in his mouth turned into something that sounded more like the roar of a desert lion protecting his cubs. With an upraised fist and that mighty yell, he flew toward his wife and toward danger.

CHAPTER SEVENTEEN

The sudden appearance of three men from the early-morning shadows of the forest, combined with the odd roar of someone on the road behind them, all served to terrify the little family and Zarah as well. They huddled together instinctively, the children pushed into the center of the ring of three adults. Zarah held the middle child, and the little girl of perhaps six years old hugged her legs, trembling.

The three men circled them quickly. One of them held a stubby knife in his grip. One of them eyed the husband, but the other was distracted by the pounding hoofbeats approaching.

Before Zarah had time to react with anything more than protection of the children, the rider on horseback, still yelling, reached the group swinging a staff, and knocked the knife-wielding attacker to his back.

"Noah!" She stood, openmouthed, as the man on the ground moaned and lay still.

Her husband leaped from his horse, barely glancing at her, staff now raised threateningly against the other two men.

The timid husband seemed to sense at once that the odds had shifted significantly. With Noah's arrival and one on the ground, there were two of them to fight the two bandits. He stepped out from his family to join Noah.

Zarah pulled the wife and the children back toward the cart while the four men took stock of each other.

The husband was a small-statured man, but the two remaining thieves were paunchy and slow, with one of them moving with a noticeable limping gait, caused by a strangely turned foot.

"You'd best be moving along, if you don't want to end up like your friend." Noah jabbed the end of the staff toward one of the men.

"We're not leaving without what we came for."

Noah stepped toward Zarah, shielding her.

The man with the twisted foot barked out a sharp laugh. "Don't worry. She's no good to us. Far past her breeding years, I'd guess."

The young wife beside her whimpered quietly.

With good reason, Zarah thought, as the men turned their attention on the woman.

"Yes, we'll definitely take that one."

But the taller thief circled around to get a better look at Zarah again, half-hidden now behind Noah.

"I don't know, Enlil. The old man seems very keen on protecting this one. Perhaps she's the one with the money."

"We're not here for money, Utu. We get what's been ordered, and we get out. You know the instructions."

Zarah narrowed her eyes. Not interested in money? What kind of bandits were these?

The women. All the missing women. Were these men responsible? They seemed barely able to think for themselves.

Now was not the time for pondering possibilities, however.

Noah lunged at the half-lame man with the end of his staff, catching the man in the gut.

The other man grabbed at the staff, and pulled, nearly yanking it from Noah's grasp.

They both gripped an end, fighting for control over the wooden pole.

With his friend occupying Noah, the faster of the two came for her.

She stepped away from the child now, and the girl ran to her mother. Zarah looked to the husband for help, but he now stood with his little tribe behind him, arms raised at his sides.

He would not be leaving them to defend her.

Zarah's hand went instinctively to the pouch at her waist.

Her attacker grabbed both her wrists and pried her arms apart, leaving her midsection vulnerable.

"And what are we hiding, old woman?"

Over his shoulder, she could see Noah still struggling for control of his staff.

She stared the man in the eyes. "As you said, I'm no good to you."

With a movement faster than she expected, he gripped both her wrists in one hand, spun her around, and pulled her to his chest. With his free hand, he reached under her tunic to grab at her chest and belly.

The violation and the humiliation brought stinging tears to her eyes.

He found the pouch beneath her tunic at once, yanked it free of the cord at her waist, and shoved her to the ground beside the first attacker, who still lay prone where Noah had felled him.

"Ah, now this is a surprise." The jewels clinked softly as they fell from the pouch into his palm.

Zarah got to her knees and was about to stand when she caught a glimpse of the knife in the dirt beside the unconscious man. She clutched at it with a sweat-slicked palm, climbed to her feet, and straightened her tunic, the knife hidden at her side.

Behind the man, Noah had finally wrested control of the staff and, with a swing at his opponent's feet, easily took the lame man's legs out from under him. He went down with a grunt.

Noah swung his staff like a scythe reaping grain, but he was too far from the taller thief to make contact.

The jewel thief seemed to sense his danger, weigh his options, and decide on the more prudent choice. Jewels clutched in his hand, he ran in the direction of the city before Noah could take him down.

Zarah still held the knife, but it would do her no good if she could not outrun him.

Both injured men were now scrabbling to their feet, and with Noah welding a staff and she a knife, they both held up palms and backed away from the group.

Neither she nor Noah would advance on the men, but they didn't know that.

"Your friend has cheated you of your profits." Noah jutted his chin toward the fleeing man. "He runs off with a sack of my wife's jewels. No doubt he'll have it spent before you see him again."

The two men must have taken Noah's speech as implicit permission to run, because they both started after their friend, one of them with his slow limp, and the other still half-bent at the waist from the undoubtedly broken ribs caused by Noah's swinging staff.

When all three had disappeared from view, the little group breathed a collective sigh of relief.

Noah gripped Zarah's arms. "Are you hurt?"

She shook her head. "Only my pride. You?"

"I am fine."

She hung her head. "The jewels. Noah, I am—"

"We will speak of it later." He turned to the family. "Are you all unhurt?"

The husband scowled. "We had no trouble until your wife joined us!"

Zarah gasped. Noah had saved their lives, and this was their thanks?

"Well, she will be leaving you now. Unless you want to travel home with us, for your own safety."

He shook his head. "We are going to Tikov, and we will reach there by midday, if the gods are willing and smile upon us."

Noah growled and opened his mouth to speak.

Zarah touched his arm to silence him. There was no point.

He nodded once and turned away. "Get your horse, Zarah. We are going home."

She untied Ibal from the family's cart, feeling nothing but shame and regret, mounted to Ibal's back, and followed Noah toward home, leaving the family to continue their journey toward Tikov.

Would they reach the city safely?

But then, what was safety, when the end of all things was near?

The children too, God? Must everything perish in what was to come? She could only pray for mercy for the children who were too young to understand their need for it.

They rode in silence for a time that stretched to such length that Zarah thought her heart would break. She could think of nothing to say. Noah knew now that she had secreted jewels from him. Knew that she had foolishly lost them as well.

She looked sideways at him through the morning, wondering if the bruises on his face and arms hurt as badly as it seemed they must.

"Your bruises…they have purpled so soon. And I barely saw that lame man lay a hand on you."

Noah grunted but did not answer at once. When he did, his voice was low and tight. "The bruises were not given by that idiot."

"Then who?"

"Barsal and his five sons."

"What?" Zarah drew her horse to a stop.

Noah continued on a few paces but finally stopped as well and circled Hazir.

"We needed the money. And we had no other means, did we?"

His words were like a jab of his staff. She had kept her jewels secreted and forced him to approach Barsal and take this beating. "Our sons?"

"Bruised and bloody as well, but alive."

She breathed a prayer of thankfulness.

"I—I do not know what to say, except that I am sorry. I thought that we would get the money from Barsal without violence. That I could save my jewels for the next emergency."

"Yes, well. Things do not always work the way you think."

With that, he turned Hazir's head back toward home and continued in heavy silence.

It was nearly nightfall by the time they rounded the last bend and saw their home in the distance.

Zarah had never been so glad to see it.

CHAPTER EIGHTEEN

Zarah awoke with an ache in her head that felt like the pounding of one of Noah's mallets against the joints of his ship. She rolled over on her sleeping mat with a groan and threw an arm over her eyes to block the incoming dawn.

A moment later, however, she was rising from her mat. After yesterday, she was not about to be caught sleeping late and skipping preparations for the morning meal.

But when she reached the rooftop, Na'el and Aris were already at work, stirring a hot mash of meat and vegetables over the fire. They both looked up at her approach.

"You are back!" Aris smiled but then snuck a sideways glance at Na'el, as if afraid of her sister-in-law's judgment. She went back to her stirring, head down.

Na'el's eyebrows were arched over wide, innocent-looking eyes. "Did you have a good journey, Mother?"

Zarah had no doubt both women already knew the entire story. She had escaped to her sleeping room the moment they returned last night, but she could hear Noah's lowered voice speaking to their sons, who certainly had conveyed the information to their wives.

She inhaled and drew her shoulders back. "It was not what I had hoped, but I am happy to be home."

Another quick smile from the loyal Aris, but Na'el was not finished with her.

"Yes, of course, we are happy to have you home as well. There is so much work to be done. None of us can shirk our duties, can we?" She finished her question with a plop of the stirring spoon onto the mat.

"No, indeed." Zarah crossed the rooftop, sat beside Aris on the mat, and reached for the spoon. "In fact, I was thinking on that very thing as I traveled home yesterday."

"Were you? That is…interesting."

Zarah gritted her teeth against Na'el's subtle insolence. "Yes. Actually, I've been thinking that it is time we women helped with the preparing of the ship."

She glanced up in time to see Na'el's mouth drop open.

"As you said, Na'el, there is so much work to be done. And since Noah believes that the One God will have us be upon the ship soon, I believe it is time for us to assist."

"But we have no skill at building! You do not expect me to swing a mallet—"

"I would expect you to do whatever is required of you by the One God." She smiled at Na'el. "However, I'm certain God would ask something more suited to you, such as carrying the clay jars of food supplies we have been saving into the storerooms of the ship."

Aris giggled, then bit her lip.

The men emerged at the stairs at that moment, all together as if they had been conferring in the lower part of the house. Salbeth appeared on the stairs behind them, calling Shem's name. Her husband turned and grabbed the large amphorae of water she had brought from the well.

Noah pulled a bench to the side of the rooftop, sat, and leaned back. "I've brought us all here to speak of what must come next."

The brothers ranged across the rooftop, with Japheth joining Aris on her mat and the others leaning against the half wall surrounding the flat roof.

Ham spoke before his father could continue. "We are finished with battling townspeople, I can tell you that." He rotated his shoulder, as if it were still sore from the beating taken at the hands of Barsal's sons.

Zarah felt the familiar twinge of guilt and looked down at her hands.

Na'el snorted. "You are blessed that you were not killed. And for what? A little money that could have been had if—"

"Enough." Noah stopped the flow of words before it finished.

Zarah knew what they were all thinking. If she had given the jewels to Noah or her sons to sell days ago, before the city had decided to cut them off, the altercation would not have happened. Nor would Noah have lost yet another day of work, chasing after her. And all for nothing.

Shem crossed his arms over his bulky chest. "She's right, Father. We could have used those jewels to buy supplies—"

Salbeth put a hand on her husband's arm. "She was only trying to help."

"But she did not help! She cost us time and gained us nothing!"

"Exactly!" Na'el nodded.

Japheth tossed a piece of barley flatbread at Na'el's basket. "Na'el, you would believe the worst of anyone, no matter the situation."

The woman picked up the bread and threw it back, hitting Japheth in the shoulder. The flatbread bounced and landed in one of the buckets of water that Salbeth had brought.

Shem grunted. "Have some regard, Na'el!"

She turned on Shem. "I thought you were on my side!"

Zarah could stand it no longer. "Stop! Just stop!" She scrambled to her feet, fists on her hips. "I am sick to death of the arguing and the disrespect! None of you understands a thing!"

Feeling suddenly nauseated, she fled down the steps, through the front room, and out into the air.

She paced close to the back of the house, where she would be unseen by those on the roof unless they peered directly over the edge. She would have run across the fields themselves, if she hadn't been certain of everyone's anger at her disappearing once again.

How could she have been so wrong? She had cost them time and money and the energy taken by their injuries. She had put them all at risk. Had made mistakes.

Wanting to do something with her hands, she crossed to the well. They would need more water before the day was through. She might as well draw it now. Her hands moved unthinking to tie the cord around the deep jar, lower it into the stone-rimmed pit, hand over hand until she heard the light *plink* of the jar against the water's surface. She let the cord go slack until it slipped against her palm as the jar began to sink, then tightened her grip and began to pull it up.

Halfway up, she nearly lost her grip. The energy seemed to have all drained out of her. She sank to her knees and kept pulling until the jar finally emerged, then stood to finish pulling it out. Exhausted, she lowered herself to the knee-high stone rim of the well, with the jar positioned between her knees.

The water shifted on the surface of the jar's wide mouth, reflecting the gray-blue sky. A bird flew overhead, its dark shadow mirrored in the water. She leaned farther, until her own face was a blurry image looking back at her.

She rarely looked at her own reflection, and today she touched a hand to her face, to her hair. The image was too indistinct to note the deepening of lines, the graying of her hair that she knew to be there. Instead, she saw only the woman she had always seen.

The woman who valued peace and harmony in her family above all else, and who was the cause of the opposite of late.

She had tried so hard to help her husband, and it was tempting to sink into self-pity at the way her good intentions had gone wrong. But she could also see that all her efforts stemmed from a lack of trust.

The problem was not her lack of trust in Noah, or even in her sons. The problem went deeper, to a lack of trust in the One God who had promised to keep them safe in whatever was to come. And though she could not see how this would happen, how the provision of money and food and supplies would be given, nor how the animals they were required to take would be collected, nor even how the ship itself would be built soundly enough to protect them, the One God was calling her to trust Him for provision and protection.

She had been like the sheep stealer in Noah's childhood story. Not shaking her fist at God's justice but shaking her head at His provision, determined to solve the problems her own way.

She leaned away from the water jar, not wanting to see herself so clearly anymore. And yet perhaps clarity and repentance were needed most.

Salbeth was there a moment later, sitting beside her on the rock rim, putting an arm around her.

"Everyone regrets their harsh words, Mother. They know you were only trying to help. Please, come back to the rooftop and hear Father's plan."

She leaned her head against Salbeth's shoulder in a brief moment of gratitude for her kindness, then nodded. "Yes, I will come. I have some things to say as well."

That evening, by the time the family had dispersed to their separate quarters, she was able to lie down beside Noah in peace. She had spoken her apologies to the family, whispered her repentance to the One God, and resolved in her heart to listen more, to focus on obedience rather than solutions.

Noah had given them all their tasks. It was time to begin the final preparations.

And she would be at his side, ensuring that her family worked together in peace, all of them, to be ready for whatever God brought them next.

CHAPTER NINETEEN

Zarah awoke to a sense of hopefulness. Together, they could finish this family project. And whatever happened—whether Noah was right about the end of all things or they continued to be a mockery to all those who watched—she would be at his side, ensuring their family worked together.

All these years, Noah had been planning and working. When the words of the Voice had first come to him, he had sat and scratched at a wet clay tablet with a sharpened fishbone for days, making lists and plans and calculations.

And for all these years, they had carried out his plans. Not only in the building of the ship but in the laying up of provisions for what was to come, by storing what grain and wine they could spare. And of late, in this last harvest as the completion drew near, storing some of the vegetables dug from the ground and the other edible plants that could be dried.

And today, today they would begin to make use of all those preparations.

She rose at daybreak.

Noah groaned at the sound of her moving in the room, rolled over, and opened one eye.

"It cannot be morning already?"

She gave him a resolved smile. "It is morning, old man. Time to turn your face to the work of the day."

It was a phrase she had used many times over the years of their marriage. Each new day was certain to bring much work and many challenges. Today even more so.

He grunted again and reached for her.

She let herself be pulled to him, warming to the affection, and lay beside him for a few precious moments.

"Come on." She slapped his thigh. "We cannot lie here all day."

"Can we not?" He clung to her.

After the sharp words and then the silence of the past two days, his words threatened to bring tears. She turned her face into his shoulder, closed her eyes, and said nothing.

"No matter what happens," he whispered, "we will have each other."

She nodded, unspeaking.

"We have each other, and we have our family. It will be enough."

She exhaled, willing his words to be true, breathing a prayer to the One God that her husband was right, that it would be enough.

The family broke bread together on the rooftop in the growing daylight.

Zarah knelt in the center of the group, ladling porridge from the pot over the cook fire into clay bowls in the hands of each.

"How long, do you think, Father?" Shem's question was one Zarah had wanted to ask. Probably all of them were thinking the same.

He shook his head. "I have had no word. I only feel that it will be soon."

He looked over the rooftop toward the ship. "And I have no idea how we will do it."

Japheth shrugged. "We can repair the fire's damage in little time. And then we are almost done with the outside of the ship. The rest could be done from inside, if necessary. After we are inside."

Noah nodded thoughtfully. "This is true. But you are forgetting what else remains to be done."

Zarah straightened. "The girls and I will open the storehouse today. We will begin to bring the provisions onto the ship."

The posture of each of the daughters drooped. No doubt each one was thinking of the backbreaking labor required to carry all those stores.

"That is good, Zarah. We will pray you have the strength to bring it all. But then, then there are…"

He broke off with a deep sigh.

Ham finished his sentence, his voice also grim. "Then there are the animals."

A few moments of silence blanketed them.

Noah spoke first. "Yes. The animals. Pairs of every living thing. *Every living thing.*" His voice thickened. "I simply do not know how we will do it."

Again the silence, but this time it was Zarah who broke in. "The birds."

All eyes turned to her.

"Yes, the birds as well." Noah nodded. "It is impossible."

"Exactly!" She smiled.

Na'el huffed. "Would you have us snatch the birds from the very air, Mother?"

Zarah turned her smile on Na'el. "It is impossible, as Father says. And so, what happens when the One God says that something will happen that is impossible?"

Noah's head lifted, a new light beginning in his eyes. "The One God must do it Himself."

Zarah nodded, a strange flutter of joy in her chest.

Noah inhaled, his chest expanding, and eyed the group. "Mother is right! Do you not see it? We could never find every living thing ourselves. Never snatch birds from the very air. Never even know if we had finished collecting them all. The One God never said we must. He only said we must bring them into the ark with us!"

"He will bring them, then?" Salbeth sat beside Noah, and her words were quiet. "He will bring them all to us? Even the birds?"

Noah flung an arm around her shoulders and squeezed. "Only three things did He ask of me. Build the ark. Bring the animals into it. Bring food for us and them. So yes, He will bring the animals, Daughter. He will bring them all."

They finished their meal hurriedly, with the unspoken understanding that the day held too much work for them to be lingering on the rooftop.

Noah and the other men left for the ship, and Zarah instructed the girls to each fetch a torch and bring it to the storehouse door.

Minutes later, Zarah pried open the small door wedged into a low hill not far from the ship and began the descent into the vast room Noah and her sons had dug underground many years ago.

The girls followed, torches in hand, down into the earthy coolness of the room.

It had been many months, perhaps a year, since Zarah had entered the storeroom with a torch. Long ago it had begun to fill, and the light filtering down from the slanted doorway was enough to see what space the floor still held for the increasing number of sealed amphorae and storage baskets coated with pitch to keep out the moisture.

Now, she directed Aris to wind her way through the narrow channel of empty floor down the center of the storeroom, all the way to the back wall, where a deep hole had been punched in the earth to hold a torch.

Salbeth and Na'el did the same with their torches, one on each side of the storeroom.

And then the four women stood back and surveyed.

Zarah inhaled sharply and fought the rising panic in her chest.

The sight of all the provisions that needed to be moved was like awakening to the work of a month of mornings, all rolled into one. If Noah was right and the time was short, could they move all this in time?

The others must have been thinking the same. None spoke.

The air smelled of dust and grain. She sniffed. Was that a hint of mildew? Her stomach clenched. Mildew would be their worst enemy in all this grain.

Na'el abruptly sneezed, followed a moment later by a sneeze from Salbeth.

"Well," Zarah said, trying to sound positive, "it must be done."

They organized quickly, bringing Ibal and the cart near to the storehouse door, forming a line from within the room, up the earthen ramp, to the cart. They began with the wine and baskets nearest the entrance, alternating between the muscle-straining weight of the wine amphorae and the relatively lighter weight of the baskets.

The cart filled slowly, with countless trips back and forth, and the only sound was the echoing of their grunts as they grabbed amphorae by their dusty necks and strained to lift and carry them.

The torches quickly warmed the low-ceilinged room, and Zarah felt the sweat cling to the back of her neck, trickle down her back, run from her scalp to sting her eyes. She swiped impatiently at her forehead with the back of her arm and kept moving.

Despite the backbreaking work, it felt good to be moving, to be doing something productive. The accusations of Na'el had stung more than the sweat in her eyes—accusations that she had been doing little to help the family lately. And indeed, even she knew that all her jewelry-making and arguing with Etana and attempting to sell stones in Tikov had done nothing to help them. So it was good to be proving herself once again, to be using her strength to organize the work and get it done.

The girls tended to complain and snap at each other as they worked, and as much as Zarah worked to move the provisions, she also worked to keep their spirits soothed and the mood peaceful.

When the cart was full, they walked Ibal to the ship.

Zarah tried to coax the animal up the ramp, into the bowels of the ship itself, where it would be easier to unload the cart.

Ibal snorted and whinnied and shook his head, clearly too nervous about the strange hulk of wood and the uncertain footing of the ramp. She cajoled and begged, even had Aris run for a piece of fruit to bribe him with, but he would have none of it.

In the end, they unhooked the cart and called the men, who appeared from their various work locations and pulled the cart up the ramp themselves in silence.

Once it was inside, rolled to the area where the provisions would be stored, her sons returned to work, but Noah paused.

Zarah jutted her chin in the direction of the retreating men. "They seem troubled."

He scowled. "I sent Ham for supplies earlier. We were running short. He returned quickly, with the news that everyone in Kish has been instructed to sell us nothing."

She nodded. It was as they had heard.

"What will you do?"

"We will have to improvise. Borrow from one section to finish another. Spread out the supplies."

From his tone, she sensed this was less than a good idea.

He inhaled, as if trying to summon good thoughts, and turned to her. "Have you seen Grandfather today? He is usually here, 'inspecting our work,' by now."

Zarah turned her head toward the grandfather's house, even though they were inside the ship. "I haven't seen him." A tickle of concern touched her. He had seemed so tired lately.

Na'el took a step toward the open door. "I will check on him."

"No," Noah stopped her. "You three unload the cart. Zarah will go. She needs the break."

Did she look as tired as she felt?

"I'm fine. Na'el can go—"

He shook his head and moved a strand of her hair out of her eyes. "You go."

She nodded in gratitude. "I won't be long."

She might have run across the field, to return and be useful sooner, but her legs would not cooperate. Not after the morning of up-and-down that earthen ramp. She tried to enjoy the fresh air and sunshine as she crossed the field.

At the door to his house, she called in. "Grandfather?"

It was dark inside the tiny home and smelled of unwashed skin.

She found him on his sleeping mat, breathing shallow and a bit raspy.

"Grandfather!" She knelt at his side and grasped his leathery hand. It was cool to the touch. Not feverish. But perhaps too cool.

"Ah, daughter. I knew you would come." He returned her handclasp, so weakly she barely felt it. "It is time, my girl."

Her heart thudded. "Time for what?"

In the dim light, she saw the gentle smile on his lips. "It is time for me to go back to Eden."

CHAPTER TWENTY

Zarah held Methuselah's frail hand to her lips. "Not yet, Grandfather. Not yet." She would have kept him for another hundred years, though she knew it was not to be. "You must wait for Noah."

He closed his eyes and gave the briefest of nods. "I will wait."

This time she did run, despite her aging legs and her exhaustion. She ran all the way, arriving at the ship and climbing the ramp with heaving breaths.

The three girls had made little progress on emptying the contents of the cart onto the shelves and storage areas built for provisions.

"What is it, Mother?" Salbeth was at her side in a moment, hands on Zarah's shoulders. "Is it Grandfather?"

She nodded, unable to speak.

Aris appeared behind her. "I will tell the men." She ran for the stairs at the end of the ship.

Even Na'el's heart seemed softened. She brought Zarah a jug of water. "Here, drink. Sit and rest."

Zarah leaned against the cart and took a swig of the water but shook her head. "There is no time to rest."

Salbeth hugged her. "He lives, still?"

"Barely."

Aris must have given the news before the men descended. They came quickly, faces grim.

Noah led the way. "Tell us, Zarah."

"He is very weak. He says that it is time. Time for him to return to Eden."

Noah smiled sadly. "Always he has believed that we will one day be restored." His glance took in the entire family. "Come, we must be with him."

Zarah straightened, but then her knees betrayed her, and she nearly fell, catching herself on the edge of the cart before she went down.

"She has run all the way," Aris said to Noah.

As though she were little more than one of his timbers, Noah swept her up in his arms and carried her down the ramp.

Outside, Ibal still munched on grass near the ship, and Noah lifted her high enough to climb on his back.

The others half ran, half walked across the field, and Ibal kept time with them. Zarah clung to his mane, trying to keep her balance despite her shaking limbs.

They all crowded into Methuselah's little home, the eight of them seeming to swallow all available space. The sons and their wives made way for Noah and Zarah to step closest to his mat and sit beside him.

Zarah took up his wrinkled hand again and whispered his name.

His eyes fluttered open, watery and red-rimmed, and he smiled. In the dim light, his pale skin seemed to glow, and even the dirty tunic he always wore seemed less stained.

The sorrow she felt at the idea of losing him weighed so heavily that the heel of her hand drifted to her chest, rubbed at the ache as though it could be erased.

All these years, he had seen her and loved her, even when she felt unseen and unloved by any other. He had never made her feel she had to prove herself, never made her feel worthless.

"I have words for you, my children." His voice was scratchy and thick.

They leaned close to hear it. The words of a man about to go to earth were a sacred thing. Some used to say that the One God would speak through words at this time. Zarah believed it still.

His watery gaze turned on her. "Daughter."

She felt his hand tremble in her grasp. "I am listening."

"The past is nothing, Daughter. It is a blot to be washed away, as though it never were. You try so hard, do so much, to make them love you. To make them see you. But the One God loves and sees you. And that is enough."

She dropped her head against his hand. It was as though he had sensed her thoughts, wanted to give her this gift, to assure her that she could go on without him. She nodded against his hand, unable to speak.

"Son."

He was looking on Noah now, but his grandson only nodded, tears flowing.

"You also have worked so hard. To build the ship. But also, to change the world, to turn them back to repentance. The One God sees and commends you for it."

Noah let out a hitched breath of emotion.

"You are a righteous man. Your father knew this. He was saddened that the people did not believe, did not follow. But he always knew you did your best. And that you were righteous."

Noah was crying now, and Zarah with him. She could hear the quiet sobs of the family behind her.

"All of you, all of you serve such a great purpose, such a calling."

"We wanted you to come with us, Grandfather." It was Shem's voice, from behind Noah.

"I know, son. I know. But that was never to be." He closed his eyes and smiled slightly. "The One God has other plans for me. And I would not refuse."

They came then, one by one to speak their love over the old man, to kiss his forehead, then step aside for the next. His eyes remained closed, but he kept that gentle smile through each approach.

Noah and Zarah returned to his side when they had finished.

His eyes opened and fixed on Noah. "There is more."

"Yes, Grandfather. I am listening."

"Seven days."

Zarah glanced at Noah for the meaning, but her husband's forehead was creased in question.

"Seven days?"

"Seven days until it comes."

There was a collective gasp in the room.

"Until the end comes?" Noah's voice was a whisper.

Methuselah's nod was so slight, she nearly missed it. "Bring the seven pairs of all clean animals and a pair of all unclean. It will be seven days until the end of all things comes, and He brings rain on the earth for forty days and forty nights, until every living thing with breath in its nostrils is destroyed. You must be ready."

Noah looked to her, eyes wide, then over his shoulder at his children. Then back to Methuselah.

"We will be ready, Grandfather. The One God must help us, but we will be ready."

Methuselah smiled again, then took a surprisingly deep breath into his frail chest. "I know you will be." He exhaled, his chest deflating. "Oh…oh, there it is." Another smile. "I can see it…."

One last exhale, and he was gone.

Perhaps restored back to the Eden he so desperately wanted to see.

CHAPTER TWENTY-ONE

They buried him in the earth outside his home.

It seemed strange, tending to such a thing as a burial, to putting a man's body into the earth, when they all believed that even the earth itself would be somehow swept away in seven days.

They stood in a ring around the rectangular patch of dirt, all eyes fixed on the mounded soil, saying nothing.

What was it Grandfather had said to her? Zarah struggled to remember each word, wanting to commit them to memory, so she could bring them out like rare jewels to polish whenever she chose.

The past is nothing. It is a blot to be washed away, as though it never were.

Had he known? All these years, had Grandfather known of her past? Somehow Barsal had known, for how long it was impossible to say. Perhaps Methuselah had heard rumors recently. Or, knowing the old man and his secrets, perhaps he had always known.

You try so hard, do so much, to make them love you. To make them see you. But the One God loves and sees you. And that is enough.

These were the words she must cling to, must remember.

A wave of fatigue washed over her, deeper than a tiredness from running across the field, or even an exhaustion borne of grief. This was a weariness that went to her innermost being. She was afraid to give way to the feeling, afraid of what would happen if she let it have free rein over her.

Why couldn't they all simply live out their lives, to their old age, and then die a natural death, surrounded by those who loved them, who would listen to final words and stoop to give kisses, and then stand round the mounded earth and weep? Was this not the way it was supposed to be?

But these were not questions any of them could answer, and the weight of Methuselah's *seven days* was a crushing force on all of them.

Noah whispered a prayer over the earth, and they shuffled away, back to the ship.

Back to the work.

The men moved faster and soon outpaced them.

Zarah led the women. "We will work in shifts," she said. "Three of us moving provisions and readying the living quarters inside the ship, while the other works in the house to prepare meals for us all. We cannot work without food. But we will take turns working inside the house, doing the less strenuous tasks."

None of the girls voiced an argument. Perhaps they were all in accord at last, now that the time was so short.

"It may mean working late in the night," she warned. "Even after we have all the provisions moved, I'm not sure what the men will need, to finish the building and be ready."

And so, they worked. The sun rose to burn the tops of their heads, and their hands grew rough and calloused from carrying the gritty amphorae. The sun set and rose again, and they repeated the day.

The cart was emptied, filled, emptied again, and brought rumbling up the wooden ramp once more to be unloaded.

Zarah worked almost without thinking, her sense of time evaporating with the sweat on her neck, and grief gnawing at her chest.

She stood beside the last enclosure to be filled with provisions, waiting for the men to pull the cart as close as possible.

Noah still worked on the roof, but her three sons were enough to haul the cart.

She was watching the muscles strain in their arms, the cords of their necks stand out, feeling proud of the boys she had raised. She was not watching how close the cart drew to where she stood.

Until the front edge of the cart rolled against her hand, pinning it to the enclosure wall.

She yelped in pain.

The boys seemed to sense the problem immediately and rolled the cart backward.

"Mother," Japheth leaped forward. "Let me see."

"It's nothing." She held her aching hand against her chest. "Only a bruise."

"Let me see."

She held out the hand and let him satisfy himself that there was no break.

"Go," she said. "We will unload."

They returned to their posts and the women began unloading, but Zarah's hand throbbed.

And somehow the pain broke through her resolve to resist the emotion that had threatened.

The tears came quietly at first but then turned to sobs.

Until she was bent over with weeping. Weeping first for Methuselah. Then weeping for Etana. Then for every person who in mere days—days!—would be destroyed.

How could they go on with the grief of the whole world on their hearts?

The girls were kind. Thankfully, Na'el was taking a turn in the house and not there to see her weakness. Aris and Salbeth led her to a bench built into the side of the ship. Brought her a cup of wine. Insisted she rest a few minutes.

She let them minister to her. She needed it.

From her place on the bench, she could see directly out of the ship through the wide door in the side, across the field that led to the city. It was not the best view to try to forget the loss of life that was to come.

Dusk was upon them, and across the field she could see the lights flickering to life. It must be lamps being lit, seen through the windows of homes. But strange that she had never noticed them so bright before. Nor so variable. They seemed to jump from window to window. She rubbed at her tearful eyes, blurring her vision further.

Aris and Salbeth crossed back and forth in front of her, obscuring her view for a few moments each time they passed.

No, the lights *were* moving. It could not be lamplight through windows.

Zarah stood, set her cup of wine on the bench, and moved across the floor of the ship to the door.

Torches. They were getting visitors, and the newcomers carried torches to light their way.

Had some in the city changed their mind? Her heart leaped at the thought. Perhaps all would not be lost! How many could they fit in this ship? Would their provisions hold long enough for more than eight?

"Girls, come!"

Aris and Salbeth joined her at the doorway.

In the growing gloom, it was hard to tell how many approached. But as the torches grew closer, she could see that only a few held them aloft. Many more joined each torch-bearer. Something about the way the mob spread sideways, half the length of the ship perhaps, touched a spark of fear in her.

"Get the men." She spoke the words without taking her eyes from the oncoming mob.

But one or all of the men must have already caught sight of the crowd from the upper level, because they were at their backs a moment later.

Noah pushed to the doorway. "Stay inside." His words were clipped, and obviously for the women.

His sons flanked him as he stomped down the wooden ramp and stood, arms folded across his chest, at its base.

"What is this? What do you want?"

Zarah could smell the burning torches from her post inside the ship. How many townspeople had come? She guessed it was a hundred or more, their tunics of all colors blending together like an angry stew. What could her family do against this multitude?

A man at the front of the crowd jabbed his torch toward the ship. "We want you to stop angering the gods!"

Shem nearly leaped forward at the man, but Noah held him back.

"And who has filled your ears with such nonsense?" Noah yelled back. "We have done nothing but *follow* the words of the One God!"

They were all shouting now. Even from her place inside the ship, Zarah could see their wild eyes and raised fists, could hear the mocking and even the curses hurled at them.

What had they done to cause such hatred?

They had only built a ship in a field on the edge of the city.

And then, as if in answer to Noah's question about where they had heard such foolishness, the crowd opened up and one man strode forward, torch in hand.

Zarah tasted the metallic tang of fear and gripped the side of the ship's doorway to keep herself upright. She felt herself near to getting sick, and breathed, lips parted, against the watering in her mouth.

This was where the hatred had come from. This one man. He had that power. He had the power to mold an entire city to his will. This she knew.

Because it did not matter how many years had passed. She would know that stride, that wide-shouldered outline, that whitened tunic and wrapped headdress, for all her life. Across any field.

The High Priest of Sin, from the Temple City of Tikov, had stepped out of her hidden past and arrived in her field.

CHAPTER TWENTY-TWO

Noah watched the unusually tall man in the white tunic stride through the crowd like a scythe through ripe wheat. He carried his torch as though it were a priestly staff.

Yes, clearly he was a priest. The man did not take his eyes from Noah as he walked forward.

Noah still stood with arms folded and returned the glare. No priest was going to intimidate him, not with the power of the One God protecting him.

"We have no quarrel with the temple of the moon god," Noah called before the priest had cleared the crowd.

The man smiled, but it was not the smile of a friend. It was the smile of a predator facing a weaker prey. "Oh, but the Temple of Sin has a quarrel with you, Shipbuilder."

Shipbuilder. It was the name that Barsal had called him. Not surprising that his neighbor had complained to this priest.

Noah raised his voice enough for those of the crowd that were closest to him to hear. "Take your friends and leave my field. We have done nothing to any of you."

"Again, you are wrong, Shipbuilder. You have angered the gods with your—your abomination." He angled the torch threateningly toward the ark as he spoke.

Noah half turned his head toward his son and spoke through his teeth. "Spread out. Protect the ark."

Yet even as he said it, his emotions were at war. He could not lose his sons in a fight here. Not at this last moment, with only a few days left.

Why? Why now? The unspoken words were lifted to the One God, with a trace of anger in his heart, he knew, but he could not help it.

Since the day on the path when he had rescued Zarah from her foolish attempt to solve the problem of money for supplies, Noah had vowed that he would not allow his family to come to harm, that he would do whatever was necessary to protect them all until they closed the door of the ark behind them.

And yet here he was, only three days later, putting them in danger again.

He glanced back at the ark's door and saw that the women were still holding back. Zarah was not even visible in the doorway. At least they were safe.

His sons had moved sideways in front of the ship, Shem to his left and Japheth farther down, and Ham to his right, between the door and the end of the ark where the mob had not yet advanced.

He recognized so many of these people. Had lived and worked, bought and sold among them for decades.

"Tirigan," he called out to the nearest familiar but angry face. "You know me. You know my family. We have done nothing. Do you follow this man blindly?"

"I follow the gods!" Tirigan yelled back. "And if Dagon says that Sin is angry, then I cannot afford to displease him. We have all seen and heard and felt the earth shaking and burning!"

His response received a rousing shout of agreement from those near him.

So, Dagon. The high priest from the temple in Tikov. But was it the god Sin that Tirigan spoke of displeasing, or only the high priest himself?

"And Ludari?" He tried another—a man who had once been a frequent guest in their home, and one who had strong opinions of his own. "Would you do harm to a friend, simply because a priest from a far-off city instructed you to do it?"

Ludari glanced at the priest, then back at Noah, and said nothing.

Ah, then they were not all convinced yet.

Perhaps they had come to see what the priest would do. Perhaps they could still be persuaded to go home without causing harm to his family or his ark.

"I do not ask you to believe my words about the end of all things, friends!" He lifted his voice above the crowd, hoping all could hear him. "I do not even ask you to believe that there is One God, as I and my family still believe. I only ask you to examine your hearts and see if you think it right to harm us, when we are doing nothing to harm you!"

It was a logical argument. How could they think otherwise?

The sky had darkened further in these few minutes, and now the high priest spread his arms wide and threw his head back, face turned up to the sky and torch extended.

"Come, Sin, rise above the horizon now, cast your glow upon those gathered here, and whisper your instructions to me. I will deliver them to your people."

A chill ran through Noah, from his hairline to the small of his back.

But before Dagon could deliver the words supposedly spoken by Sin, shouts from the left end of the ark drew everyone's attention.

Someone had apparently ventured toward the ark with a yell, some kind of farming tool upraised in obvious intent to damage the ark.

Shem and the other man were now locked in a struggle, with Shem holding the man's arm still aloft, too far from the ark to land a blow.

Again, the anger built in Noah's chest. Anger at the people, anger at the One God for continuing to shorten their time to obey His instructions while at the same time allowing obstacles to interfere.

"Hold, Shem!" His yell carried across the crowd, and he ran to assist his son. Japheth beat him there, and Ham arrived a moment later.

But the two-man altercation had already spread. Fists were flying, neighbors were shrieking.

Noah barreled into the center of it with a roar of his own.

The air smelled of burning tar. From the torches or the pitch coating of the ark?

He threw a punch and connected with a stranger's jaw. Spittle flew.

And then another, this time against the cheekbone of a former friend.

A fire burned in his belly at the swirling, shrieking mass of people who clotted so close to the ark, then broke apart from the four wild men protecting it, then formed again to push forward.

He lost track of how many men he had pummeled, tasted blood in his mouth from the hits he had taken.

Even the women were close enough to threaten. The scent of perfume mixed with odor of burning tar and sticky sweat.

And then one of the women—Radjni, if memory served—took a hit to the left eye from the elbow of a nearby fighter.

Radjni screamed and went down.

She would be trampled if she lay there! Noah dove into the crowd, arms reaching for her.

He formed a shield over her with his body, grabbed her wrists.

She wrapped tight fingers around his wrists, the look of terror in her eyes turning briefly to relief.

Thankfully, she was not too much a part of this insanity to resist his help. He pulled her to standing, dragged her away from the fight.

"Let me see," he held her head toward the light of a nearby torch and examined her eye. "You will have a bruise, but it will heal." He glanced at the horde still fighting. "But please, go home before it gets worse!"

She bit her lip and followed his gaze. "My husband…"

Noah exhaled. "Then at least stay here!" He guided her to the hull of the ark.

Not everyone had entered the melee. Noah could see that farther down the line, most of the mob watched.

Dagon stood in the center of the watching crowd, chin still raised in defiant arrogance.

No doubt Dagon could rouse the rest of them if he chose. Perhaps he was only waiting.

The four of them could not hold back this crowd if all were incited to anger.

He left his sons to hold as best they could and ran back toward the quieter, watching crowd.

"Neighbors, take thought! Already some of you are hurt"—he raised an arm toward the fighting—"including your women! Take your families and go home before it gets worse!"

A low murmur rippled over the crowd. Had he gotten through to them at last? Their sudden silence surprised him.

And then their upturned faces caught his attention, despite the growing darkness.

Did they also pray to the moon god?

Half worried that the moon itself was answering, he followed the collective gaze and looked to the sky.

But it was not the moon.

It was the birds.

Soaring, floating, cawing...a host of birds circled above their heads.

Not a sudden appearance of an entire flock, as sometimes traveled together over the fields or descended on newly harvested grain.

No... Birds of all kinds swooped, sang, and then landed, one by one, on the rim of the ark's roof. They stared down at the crowd with dark and piercing eyes.

Even the fighting slowed and then stopped at the sudden and unexplainable appearance of so many birds.

Dagon seemed to sense he was losing his mob. "The moon god Sin has sent birds of prey to—to—warn you—"

But his words did not take root. Perhaps if it had only been birds of prey, and not so many others. Or perhaps if Sin, a god that only appeared at night, had ever been known to send birds. Perhaps, even, if the birds had not lined the ark's rooftop and looked down like protective sentries.

But in the face of such a thing, the people did not even seem to hear Dagon.

Noah's sons joined him near the door of the ark, each of them with eyes wide, mouths agape.

And then a shriek from the back of the crowd, and the swift parting again of former friends and neighbors.

Down the parted space between townspeople walked a jackal. Slow, steady, assured of his own superiority. And then another matching animal with it.

The sight was enough to terrify anyone. But then another pair appeared out of the darkness.

Two leopards.

Two leopards. Walking through his field.

Chills once again swept Noah's body.

The anger he had felt at these people drained away, like water into parched soil.

And the anger he had felt at the One God was gone as well, replaced by a grateful sense of awe.

The animals. The animals had started to come.

As though they had been trained, the jackals approached the ark, dipped their heads in the direction of Noah and his sons, and trotted up the wooden ramp into the lower deck.

His sons' wives pulled back, no doubt in some fear but mostly shock on their faces.

The leopards followed the jackals onto the ark.

And then there were more. Trotting, walking, loping. Single file, sometimes in pairs, and sometimes in small groups, animals began pouring through the break in the crowd, toward the ark.

Those in the back of the crowd must have seen them first and began to flee.

Now the panicked flight of neighbors reached the front of the crowd, and they flowed away from the ark, like sand pouring through fingers.

Dagon held his ground, but there was an uncertain fear flickering in his expression. "Do not fear, friends!" His voice carried over the crowd. "There is nothing to fear."

But his words were lost to them, and he could not rouse a crowd that was both confused and unwilling.

"This is not over, Shipbuilder!" Dagon kept glancing at the surge of wild creatures. "Sin will not be defeated!"

Noah grinned. "Tell your moon god he'll need many more followers if he hopes to stop the One God!"

And then he turned and motioned to his sons to follow him into the ark.

It was time to see to their new visitors.

But he could feel the angry stare of Dagon, trying to burn a hole in his back. No, it was clearly not over. But for now, the One God had shown Himself more powerful.

And for now, that would be enough.

CHAPTER TWENTY-THREE

Zarah watched the crowd disperse with awe.

From her vantage point inside the ship, she had not seen the birds land on the roof, but the sight of them circling had been enough of a surprise.

When the jackals led the unlikely stream of various wild animals up the ramp and into the lower hold of the ship, she and the other women stood aside, clutching each other.

But despite the ability of many of these animals to tear them to pieces, Zarah felt little fear in their presence.

It was the man outside who caused the fear to thud like a drumbeat in her chest.

She had not seen Dagon in many, many years. Since long before her sons were born. Before she met Noah. It was like another life. One she had kept secret, with no reason to ever bring out in the light.

But he was here. Dagon was here, and her past had found her. She held tighter to the girls, willing her shaking hands to be still, fighting the nausea building in her belly like a fire.

Dagon had threatened them before disappearing into the night. Told Noah that his attack against them was not over, that he would be back.

She must do something. She knew Dagon like no one else in her family knew him. She knew how his mind worked, what it would take to convince him to leave her family alone.

Seven days. They only needed five more. All her doubts had flown away when the birds flew in. Between Grandfather's prediction and the arrival of the animals, there could be no doubt that Noah had indeed heard the Voice, and that their uncertain obedience all these years had not been in vain.

The men were trying to direct the animals into the appropriate stalls, separating kinds that would typically be predator and prey.

"Remarkable!" Noah kept saying until they all were laughing.

Aris clapped her hands together and held them to her mouth. "They do not attack each other! How is such a thing possible?"

"How is any of this possible?" Japheth hugged his wife.

Noah pointed. "Shem, use your rod to guide those... those—whatever they are—to the next deck. This level is for the largest beasts."

Shem tried to direct a jumbled group of hopping, scurrying animals up the ramp at the end of the ship.

They were all so gleeful. Zarah couldn't keep from smiling, despite her inner turmoil.

She could go to him, go to Dagon and convince him to give them a bit of time. She was the only one who could.

But she was not foolish enough to think she should, or even could, attempt such a thing without any of her family knowing.

What would the truth mean to them? What would they think of her if they knew her past?

The past is nothing. It is a blot to be washed away, as though it never were.

Perhaps the One God had somehow forgiven her, when she had called upon His mercy. But could her family forgive?

It took hours to corral all the animals that had come, and still came. When the field at last was empty and it seemed the flow had stopped and the penning was done, the family retired at last to the warmth of the cook fire on the rooftop and Na'el's crusty bread and hot lentil stew.

They ate in silence at first, all of them too famished to waste time talking. But soon the conversation began to flow, then the recounting of the amazing day, with stories growing more dramatic with each telling.

Shem's bellowing laugh lifted to the sky. "You should have seen Japheth when that man who sells the cheaper wine— what's his name? Belanum. Yes, you should have seen Japheth when Belanum came swinging at him!"

Japheth punched his brother playfully on the shoulder. "You would have ducked too if that great sack of grain came rolling toward you!"

Zarah smiled but kept an eye on Noah, watching his mood.

Finally, belly queasy with the spicy dinner and heart pounding, she broke into the conversation.

"I—I need to talk to you all about something." Her voice quavered, and she swallowed hard to strengthen it.

The chattering and laughter stilled, and their eyes turned to her.

She dropped her gaze, stared at her hands, twisted together in her lap.

"What is it, Zarah?" Noah reached across and gripped one of her hands. "Were you hurt—"

"No. No, I am fine. It is not about today. Well, it *is* about today, but not about—"

"Just tell us."

She risked a look into his eyes.

He smiled, a bit sadly, but nodded.

"It is about my life before I met you, Noah. There are things I must tell you."

Noah wiped his mouth with a cloth and glanced at the rest of the family. "Perhaps in private?"

She inhaled and shook her head. "No. No, everyone must hear this. I should have told you all long ago."

"Mother, you can tell us anything." Salbeth's kind words.

She took one more breath and plunged in.

"My parents were very poor. I was the youngest of four girls. When I was born, the disappointment was tremendous. By that time, they knew their fate was sealed. With no boys to help my father work the land, they assumed he would die young and that my mother and three sisters and I would be destitute. My parents worshipped at the moon god's temple, and they believed that three was the sacred number of Sin, and so my birth was deemed an ill omen. At the very least, unnecessary."

Noah grunted in disapproval.

So far, she had only their pity. But they had not heard it all.

"By the time I was eight, we were figuring out how to survive. Mother got sick, needed a healer, and couldn't work. The work that my sisters did helped a bit, but we were all young, and I could not do much."

Salbeth again, laying a pitying hand on her shoulder. "I am sure you did your best. But you were only a little girl."

"Yes. I was a young girl. And the temple needed young girls. And so, they sold me to the temple."

There. She had passed the point of no return now. The beginning of the truth was out there.

Silence ringed the cook fire. She didn't dare look at any of their faces. Perhaps there would be pity, but what if it was horror? Scorn?

"I—I can clearly remember the day. My father took me, alone, which was strange, because my mother always came when there was a sacrifice to offer and my sisters often came. But he lied and told me that we were making a special, secret sacrifice on behalf of my mother, to help her get better." She sniffed and wiped away a trickle of tears. "It turned out that I was the sacrifice."

"He just...sold you?" Na'el, her voice soft but indignant.

Zarah nodded, still looking at her hands. "I remember that my father seemed so angry. And the priest was yanking me from my father, even though I was clinging to him. Crying. My father's eyes were closed the entire time, and I know now that he couldn't stand to watch, but at the time it felt like he was so disgusted with me that he couldn't look at me. That I was such a disappointment. I knew how much he had counted on my being a son."

The words tumbled out on their own now, and it felt as if she were right back in that temple. "He was so angry. I assumed he was angry with *me*—for not being a son but more than that, for being…too small-boned to be a hard worker like my sister Lilith, not pretty enough to command a high bride-price like Gemekala, for being not as skilled at weaving as Iltani. I was not special. I was ordinary. I was unworthy of being his child. And so he sold me away."

Noah slid nearer to her and pulled her to himself, cradling the back of her head and lowering it to his shoulder.

She wept with abandon at the memories. How good it felt to be comforted by him!

But she pulled away moments later. "That is not all. I must tell you all."

"Finish your story, Zarah, and then let us tell you what we know you are worth."

She half smiled at Noah.

"I don't think you understand. I grew up in the temple. I served the moon god in ways I don't wish to talk about. And I got older. Old enough to make my own choices. To run away if I had wanted to do so. But I didn't. I stayed. I stayed as a priestess of Sin and served the moon god of my own free will!"

It was finally all told. There were details they didn't need to know, but they knew the most important part. That she had not always followed the One God but had once given her body and soul to the false gods of Tikov.

Noah's arm around her had grown heavy. Perhaps cold.

She pulled away, finally willing to risk a look around the circle of her family.

They stared at her, probably unable to imagine their mother a young woman, a young priestess of a false god.

Noah was moving. Climbing to his feet. He reached down to pull her to standing.

Her heart was in her throat. She held back.

"Stand up, Zarah."

She stood.

And then Noah swept her into his arms and buried his face in the nape of her neck.

They were all there a moment later, arms around her, touching her shoulders, stroking her hair.

A blot to be washed away, as though it never were.

She could barely catch her breath between the stifled sobs and the embraces. And in that moment she was able to let that horrible past slip away from her just a little bit. Not as if it had never happened, not yet, but perhaps it had loosened its grip on her.

Finally, she pulled away, wiped her face, and smiled.

"One more thing," she said.

They watched her, some with raised eyebrows as if worried about this next revelation.

"All those years in the temple—the Temple of Tikov—I served under High Priest Dagon."

She waited, but they didn't seem to understand.

"Dagon, who led that angry multitude tonight."

Ah, there was the surprise she expected.

"I grew to know him better than I'd ever known my own father. And that is why I am going to talk to him. To convince him to stop this fight against our family."

CHAPTER TWENTY-FOUR

Zarah's pronouncement was met with silence once again. It would seem she had not stopped surprising them.

Noah finally found his voice. "Zarah, that is foolishness! The man is evil."

She shrugged. "Perhaps. But as I said, I know him."

"You *knew* him." Ham's arms were crossed. "It was a long time ago."

She smiled. "Not as long as it probably seems to you. To me, it was…" Her vision darkened for a moment at the memories, but she tried to shake them off. "I know how to talk to him. I can convince him to go back to Tikov. To leave us alone."

Silence again, as if each of them were trying to find a good argument but not succeeding.

"Then I am going with you. I won't let you walk into that viper's nest alone." Noah scratched at his beard. "We will leave at first light."

"No." Zarah's voice held firm. "You may come if you wish, but we leave now. Before this goes any further, before Dagon concocts any more schemes against us, and before tomorrow comes with whatever the One God plans to bring us next!"

Noah's lips parted slightly, and his eyebrows rose. "As you wish, Wife."

"We are not letting the two of you go alone, either," Shem said. "You will have the three of us with you as well."

His brothers nodded in agreement.

"And we will not stay here alone!" Na'el's voice was pitched even higher than usual. "Not with that ship full of wild animals so close!"

Zarah breathed deeply and looked around the circle. "Very well. Dagon will receive eight visitors tonight." She waggled a finger at each. "But you will let me do the speaking."

She hadn't talked to her sons like they were children in many years. They smiled at her tone.

Extra cloaks were donned, and they were off, across the dark field and toward the city.

"How will we know where to find Dagon?" Aris whispered, as though the high priest could hear them from the street.

"He will be at Kish's temple, though it is nothing so grand as the one in Tikov. Still, the priest here has doubtless given him a place to sleep." Zarah spoke as if knowledgeable about temple matters, and she sensed the wonderment of her children still.

From the street, the tiny Temple of Kish seemed little more than a mud-brick building with some carved statues at its doors.

Zarah led the way to the door, and they passed two priestesses who watched them enter with wide eyes. The eight passed through to the inner courtyard, smoky with burning torches surrounding a central altar.

Nothing burned on the altar tonight, but orange embers still glowed, a mute testimony to a recent sacrifice.

Another priestess entered the open courtyard and stopped when she saw the eight assembled there.

"We wish to speak to Dagon." Zarah's voice rang clear through the courtyard.

The woman's forehead creased. "What are you doing here?"

"Do you know who we are?"

Her eyes darted to take them all in, and a bit of fear perhaps flitted across her face. "I know who you are."

"Then you know that Dagon will wish to speak to us."

Still she lingered. "Why does your husband stay mute?"

Zarah tilted her head at the girl. "Tell Dagon that an old friend has come for a visit."

At that, the girl shook her head slightly and moved into the shadows.

Zarah turned to her family and welcomed the support she saw in their eyes.

When Dagon entered the courtyard, Zarah *felt* his presence before she saw the man himself.

Back at the ship, she had stayed hidden, not wanting Dagon to know she was Noah's wife, and hadn't been able to see him clearly.

Now he stood before her, significantly aged by the years that had passed, but still with such darkness about him.

Her knees shook under her long tunic, and she gripped Noah's hand. Something bitter surged up into the back of her throat.

"Dagon." She licked her dry lips. "It has been a long time."

Dagon crossed the courtyard, staring at her face. "Zarah? Is this truly Zarah?"

She was somewhat gratified to see a look of vague pleasure on his features.

"I—I never thought to see you again. As you say, it has been a long time." He had composed himself already, taking in the seven people behind her. "I see you have found a new family to belong to." He wrinkled his nose. "And a different sort of family, indeed."

"You were never my family, Dagon."

He pursed his lips. "Oh, Zarah, you are unkind. What did I ever do but treat you like a daughter?"

She felt Salbeth lean against her, as if to give her courage.

The fire that had been in her belly since she first saw him flamed hotter for a moment. "Daughters are more of a treasure than you could ever understand." She wrapped an arm around Salbeth's waist. "And you were never a father to me."

"More of a father than your own, I daresay."

She refused to be baited into forgetting her purpose.

"I have come to speak to you on behalf of my family. About our ship."

He laughed. "Yes, your *ship*. Such a foolish mockery of a thing. A ship in the middle of a field."

"If it is so foolish, why does it warrant a visit from the high priest? And not a visit only, but a rounding up of half the city to come against us as if we are their enemies?"

He stretched his neck, studied the sky, but said nothing.

"As you say, Dagon, we are nothing more than fools. Certainly, it is beneath you to even spend a fraction of your attention on us."

He brought his gaze back to hers, piercing her through in a way that brought back unpleasant memories. She tried to return the look but felt herself shaking again.

Salbeth's arm went around her back, and Noah stepped close to her side.

"It is not for me to say, Zarah, why the god Sin is displeased with your little family and their ridiculous ship. I can only tell you that the god wishes for it to be destroyed."

"Then your god wishes to destroy all of humanity."

He laughed again. "Ah, yes, I have heard this story. The 'end of all things' is coming, and only those who are aboard your ship will be saved. Did I get that right?"

Noah spoke for the first time, stepping in front of Zarah. "That is right, Dagon. The One God has wearied of the rebellion of mankind and is going to destroy the earth."

"Well, then, you have nothing to fear from me, do you?" Dagon tapped a hand against the side of the altar. "You have the 'One God' as you say, on your side. What can I do to fight against that?"

"Give us seven days, Dagon." Zarah kept her voice as sweet as she could. "For the sake of our former—friendship. Give us seven days, and then if the end does not come, we will begin to dismantle the ship."

This was the argument she had prepared before coming. Dagon valued logic, but he also loved a bargain. How could he resist such an easy solution to what he saw as a problem?

She could feel her family shuffle and murmur in displeasure at the deal she offered. But she was putting all her faith in the One God. And He had said seven days.

Dagon shrugged. "We shall see." And then he spun on his heel and was gone.

It was the best they could have hoped for. Zarah led the way out of the temple, into the street, and back toward their home.

They could hear the sounds of the animals before they'd reached the house, a welcome reminder that the One God was with them.

With hearts full of the day's drama, they each found their mats and slept until the first light broke across the field.

Zarah awakened to a little squeal coming from the front room. She scrambled to her feet, closely followed by Noah.

"Aris, what is it?"

The girl stood at the door, mouth open. "More!"

They joined her at the door.

If yesterday's steady stream of animals had been amazing, the sight that faced them now was downright shocking. The entire field was filled with animals, moving in slow procession toward the ship.

They dressed hurriedly, all of them, and did not stop to break bread. It was Salbeth's turn to remain in the house to prepare meals, and she handed each of them a hunk of bread as they passed through the door to get to work.

The morning passed in what felt like minutes. The women dealt with the animals and continued to arrange the provisions and ready the sleeping quarters. The men worked on the outside of the ship, doing repairs and final adjustments.

Already, the feeding and care of the animals was proving to be a challenge. The women drew water from the cisterns that had been collecting rain for several weeks and parceled out the first of the provisions.

When the sun had climbed to about noon, the men entered the ship to find the women sweeping up the pens.

Noah crossed the ship swiftly, grabbed Zarah, and spun her around twice.

"What? What are you doing, you crazy old man?" She laughed, and it felt like something she hadn't done in a long time.

"The hull is finished!" Noah hooted. "This thing is as solid as it can be. Now we can finish the interior, and then we will be ready!"

Japheth's stomach took that moment to growl. "And I am ready for food!"

"Come," Noah said, "let's take a break and see what Salbeth has prepared for us. I hope it's a feast!"

Salbeth was not in the front room, so the seven climbed the steps to take their midday meal on the roof.

But Salbeth was not on the roof, either. No cook fire burned there. No pot of food simmered over coals, no loaves of bread had been laid out.

They looked to each other in surprise, and clear disappointment. They were all hungry.

"I will find her," Shem said, and headed back down the steps, into the house, calling his wife's name.

Zarah crossed to the edge of the roof, shielded her eyes from the sun, and scanned the surrounding fields for any sign of Salbeth. There was nothing.

Shem was back a moment later. "She's not here." He joined Zarah at the roof's edge.

"I don't see her," Zarah said.

They all searched the fields, but clearly she was nowhere close enough to be spotted.

Zarah looked to Shem. "She wouldn't have gone into the city, would she?"

"For what reason?" He shook his head. "And she would know it wasn't safe."

They all stood there, looking at each other, no one able to offer an explanation.

Shem's face grew more worried with each passing moment. "I—I don't understand what could have happened—"

"There!" Na'el was pointing across the field, toward the city. "Someone is coming."

"Is it Salbeth?" Shem leaned over the edge of the roof, as if he'd see more clearly.

They all watched in silence. Zarah chewed her lip, not wanting to think of what might have happened to Salbeth.

Moments later, it became obvious that the figure crossing the field was a man.

They waited. Whoever this was, it must be about Salbeth. Who else would come?

"It is the little priest of Kish." Shem's voice was tight. "I will go down."

He descended the steps alone.

Zarah tried to join him, but Noah held an arm against her waist, blocking her from the steps, and signaled for quiet.

They could hear the priest speaking to Shem.

"A message from Dagon," he said. "You will dismantle your ship, beginning immediately. Or the woman will be killed."

At the yell from Shem, Noah dove down the steps, followed by Shem's brothers.

Zarah kept the women on the roof, but they could hear everything.

"Dagon has the audacity to steal my wife!" Shem was shouting. "To threaten us!"

"Where is she?" Noah's voice sounded like it could cut the little priest down where he stood. "Where has Dagon taken Salbeth? Are they in your miserable temple? Because we will haul him out of there and—"

"You will not. They are gone."

"What do you mean, 'gone'?" Shem's throaty growl sounded more animal than human.

"Back to Tikov. They left hours ago, just after first light."

Zarah gasped. They must have come for Salbeth just after the family left for the ship.

Dagon had watched so carefully when Salbeth had come to her support last night in the temple. At the time, Zarah had felt gratified that the old man could see she now had family that loved her.

But what had that love gotten Salbeth?

She was now at the mercy of the very evil they fought against.

CHAPTER TWENTY-FIVE

Zarah could stay on the roof no longer.

Followed by Aris and Na'el, she hurried down the stairs.

The priest was still at the door. His eyes flicked toward her, where she stood behind Shem and Noah. "Dagon has a message for you as well." He wrinkled his nose, as if disgusted by the words he was instructed to deliver. "You have a choice. The ship, or you."

Noah edged Shem out of the doorway. "What is that supposed to mean?"

He shrugged. "It's not my place to question. But the high priest has said that if your wife will offer herself in place of the girl, the girl can leave and you can continue with your... project." Again, the wrinkling of the nose.

"Leave my house." It was Noah's turn to growl at the little man. "I said, go!"

Zarah's stomach was in a knot as Noah shut the door behind the priest and turned to face his family. Her sons were watching her as well.

She said nothing. What could she say?

Shem spoke first. "I am going after them."

Noah's gaze lingered on her a moment more, and then he looked to Shem and nodded. "The three of us will come. Perhaps we can overtake them on the road."

Ham grunted. "That's our only chance. If they make it to Tikov, we'll need more than four of us to get past temple guards and get her out."

Shem was already heading out the door. "Then we won't let them make it!"

Zarah looked to the other two women. "We will pack supplies."

Noah shook his head. "No time."

And then they were gone, leaving silence in their wake, with all three women staring at the door left ajar.

Aris finally pushed past her to run outside, and Zarah and Na'el followed to see them off.

"Come," Zarah said when the men and their horses had faded to dark smudges on the horizon, "we must continue the work."

"You would go on, as if nothing at all has happened?" Na'el's eyes burned. "Do you even care for her at all?"

Zarah bit back a reply. Care for Salbeth? She loved the girl like her own daughter. And it was her fault she'd been taken. Taken to... No, she would not think on that possibility, although ever since she had seen the high priest outside the ship last night, the pieces had begun to fall together. The disappearing women over the past few months. Dagon's plans had spread to Kish.

She must believe that Dagon had taken Salbeth only to force Zarah to return to the temple, or to force Noah to dismantle his ship. Either way, Dagon had a victory, and that was all he ever cared about.

"Na'el, you know I love Salbeth. And we will pray as we work. But Noah and your husbands would want us to continue." She grabbed a scrap of fabric from the table and tied her hair back. "Bring torches and let's get to work."

The early-morning stream of incoming animals had slowed, but there was still much work to be done to settle them in pens, begin the day's feeding, organize the provisions.

Despite her brave words, Zarah removed herself from the other two inside the ship, moved to the second level to work alone where they would not see her weeping.

How could it have come to this?

All those years ago, she had waited for Dagon to show himself in Kish, or at least send lesser priests or temple guards to search her out. But they had never come. And over time, she had come to believe that he had forgotten her or that he no longer cared about what had happened. She had remained hidden, unknown, for years. Married Noah. Raised her boys. Raised a ship.

And then that very ship had brought Dagon back to her.

The pen of goats already needed mucking out. She grabbed an iron shovel from where it stood propped against the wall of the pen and began scraping dung toward the wide aisle that ran down the center of the dark second level. How would they ever keep up with all these animals?

Her thoughts were as dark as the ship's interior and as distasteful as her task.

She had tried to focus on simple obedience. Tried not to take matters into her own hands or believe that she needed to solve everything. And then last night, when she saw Dagon and realized that she could be the one to save them all, she had so quickly raced to confront him.

And once again, her actions had brought more than failure, they had brought disaster.

Once again, she had proven herself a liability to this family rather than asset.

She shoveled her pile onto a dirty blanket, tied the four corners as best she could, and began dragging it down the ramp. Why had the One God not told Noah to cut windows into this level?

The ship smelled like a thousand animals, and the noise—the noise was enough to drive her to madness. Halfway down the ramp, she stopped to swipe at her face with the back of her arm. She was doubtless filthy but couldn't see well enough to know.

She should have gone with them. Gone with the men to face down Dagon.

No, that would have been more of the same. More trying to make herself useful in ways that only brought harm.

The blanket's knot loosened, releasing its contents to tumble down the ramp.

Zarah sank to her knees, leaned against the interior wall, and closed her eyes in defeat.

Did any of it matter anymore? Why not simply let the end come? This world was a terrible place, filled with Dagons and Barsals and all the evil one could imagine, but she and her family were just as human and why should they be preserved?

Would they not simply start the whole evil process again, when nothing was left but them?

Far better to follow Methuselah, perhaps. Back to the Garden. Or back to the earth or to wherever the life inside a person departed to when the body ceased to function.

"What are you doing there, Mother?" Aris peered up from the gloom at the bottom of the ramp.

Zarah wiped at her face again, not caring what she smeared there. "Just resting a moment."

Aris disappeared, then reappeared with a torch. She waved it over the base of the ramp. "What happened here?"

Zarah did not have the energy to reply. And besides, it was obvious. She leaned her head against the wall and said nothing.

"Na'el, come help me."

The other girl appeared. "What is she doing?"

"She is resting."

They stood there, the two of them, at the bottom of the ramp. Staring up at her.

She should tell them to keep working. She should keep working herself.

Instead, they all waited inside the dark belly of this ship, as though they had already gone to earth themselves. Dark and dank, odorous and noisy.

In the old days, when she was a priestess of the moon god Sin, there were stories of the underworld, whispered around the altar. Sometimes, late at night on her sleeping mat, she had imagined what such a place might be like.

Now she knew.

CHAPTER TWENTY-SIX

Noah's sons brought the horses, and without a change of clothes, a skin of water, or a crumb of bread, all four men mounted, turned their beasts' heads in the direction of Tikov, and kicked their mounts into a gallop without so much as a farewell.

Shem led the charge to rescue his wife, with Noah and his brothers trailing only a head length behind.

"The priest must have had servants with him. But with Salbeth also mounted, they should be slowed." Shem's eyes shone with anger. "We can overtake them, even if it takes until they stop for nightfall."

Noah said nothing, only urged his horse, Hazir, harder. He could have said that they did not know for certain where the two were taking Salbeth, so how could they know if they followed in their path? But they followed the main road out of Kish, toward Tikov. What else could they do?

They rode hard, the road cutting through fields of golden grain nearly ready for harvest, through forests that crowded close to them and spooked their horses. They splashed through marshy lowland and crested hills that blocked the sun as it dipped to the western horizon. The day had grown hazy with gray, scudding clouds, their undersides lit up with fire as the sun went down.

No sign of Dagon and his entourage.

Nothing but a few merchants traveling slowly, who edged away from the rampaging foursome, and a small family with a donkey and wagon, who stopped and watched them approach with wide eyes.

The men stopped to question both of these small groups, but none had seen a priest with a woman on horseback.

Darkness fell hard, with the sun dropping beneath the horizon and the gray sky turning inky.

"Watch for a fire," Shem said as they continued into the darkness. "They will have stopped for the night now."

They traveled only a bit slower, each scanning the sides of the road for any signs of a camp.

But several hours into the night, even Shem had slowed, giving his horse a needed respite but his own head drooping as well. "They cannot have taken this road. Or must have turned off somewhere." Shem's voice caught in his throat.

Noah drew alongside his son and gripped his shoulder. He had been loath to end this chase, but it was clear they would not find the girl tonight. "We should turn back."

Shem's muscles tightened under Noah's grip.

"We have no supplies, Shem. No money. Nothing with which to pursue this further."

Shem's head lifted toward Tikov.

Ham, who was ahead by a few cubits, circled his horse and reined him to a stop in front of the rest of them. "Father is right. We must get supplies and perhaps weapons. And more information—from Mother, who knows Dagon and the city of Tikov, and its temple."

Noah said nothing. He loved Salbeth. But his mind was on the ark, the instructions from God, the remaining four days of his grandfather's dying words, and the way the earth itself seemed to be in agreement. How could they delay the project to seek out Shem's missing wife?

They rode toward home in the darkness, none of them willing to make camp with nothing to sleep on, nothing to cover them, nothing to eat. Better to keep moving, with the promise of their beds and a hot meal ahead.

In the silence broken only by the *clop* of horses' hooves, Noah had time to think, to pray to his God, and to ask questions.

Why was this happening now? Now when they were so close to finishing? Was the One God mocking him? Testing him?

The people of Tikov worshipped Sin and a host of other dark and angry gods. Most of them would have said that Noah's God was toying with him, making sport out of giving him irrational instructions that must be obeyed, and then thwarting him with dishonest neighbors who would not pay for their purchases, and upper decks that splintered into ruins, and daughters who were stolen away for no reason.

Is that the way in which his own God worked?

He had tried so hard, all his life, to refute the idea that the One God was as the angry gods of sun and moon, earth and rain, that the people futilely worshipped. His family had held to the truth. Tried to remain pure in the midst of the darkness. No, more than that—they had tried to *fight* the darkness. To eradicate it. To spread the truth.

And they had failed.

He had failed. He and all his fathers before him had failed.

And now the failure was so great that the world itself must be destroyed.

The aching sadness never left Noah's chest. It was like a stone that could not be dislodged. A binding that sometimes made it hard to breathe. From his birth he wanted nothing more than to save the world. Instead, he was being asked to stand by and watch while it was destroyed.

Well, at least he would not fail in this. Not in this.

And so, in the early hours of the morning, as they left the last forest behind and entered the fields outside of Kish, he spoke the words he'd been dreading all night to speak.

"We must keep building, sons."

They were the first words spoken in hours, and the three men turned drowsy heads and bleary eyes to him, as though none of them comprehended his words.

"The days grow short, and God's instructions were clear. We must keep building. Finish the ark."

Shem's eyes narrowed, his forehead creased. "What are you saying, Father?"

"I am sorry, my son. I love her too. But we cannot take the time—"

"No!" Shem shoulders flared back. "There is no way that I am going back to your foolish ship when my wife—"

"We cannot finish without you. The work is too much, even for four of us, I fear."

Shem's jaw set, and his glare was enough to set the fields aflame. "You cannot be serious, Father. All these years I have labored by your side, without a word from your God, without questioning what you think you heard. And now you would choose this—this—*ship*—over Salbeth? And ask me to do the same?"

Noah exhaled, sadness and fear and a bit of shame pressing against his chest now. "Shem—"

But Shem was clucking to his horse, goading its flanks with his heels. And then flying toward home.

Ham and Japheth both looked to Noah, not speaking but with expressions that said nearly as much as Shem. And then they urged their horses faster to follow their brother.

Noah let Hazir take his time. Shem wanted to make plans for his next chase. Ham and Japheth had wives who waited for them. Noah was in no hurry to get back.

CHAPTER TWENTY-SEVEN

From her place on the rooftop, Zarah heard the men returning before they emerged from the early-morning gloom.

She had tossed on her sleeping mat for several hours before
giving up and coming to the roof, to think under the stars and
pray for Noah and his sons to return with Salbeth, unharmed.
The cold hours had been spent in prayer, yes, but mostly in
reminiscing. The memories were not happy.

And now, watching for the horses, praying for the best, she
pushed aside the memories in hopes that it would not be necessary to resurrect them again.

Only three horses appeared along the road. Zarah's heart
thudded in her chest. Who was missing? She squinted, leaned
over the half wall of the rooftop, traced the outline of each
man with her gaze.

Shem at the lead, his broad shoulders bent forward, urging
his horse.

Ham and Japheth behind him, one taller and the other
more slight, both dark-haired.

Noah. Missing.

And Salbeth not with them.

Zarah swallowed against the bitterness in her throat and
chest.

Had they encountered the priest? Had Noah been harmed, and Salbeth with him?

She counted the steps of the returning men, fingers tapping against the wall. Willing herself to remain here on the roof until they were nearly home. There was no sense in running out to them. The news would not change between here and there.

But wait! Another figure, at the edge of her vision. A fourth rider, coming along behind, slower than the others.

Thoughts of waiting forgotten, Zarah ran to the steps, down and out of the house, across the field until she reached Shem.

"What news? Did you see them? Salbeth?"

Shem shook his head. "No sign of them. We returned for supplies and information. We will leave at first light tomorrow."

Zarah peered into the dawn, now coming up behind the solitary figure of Noah in the distance. "Your father? Is he unhurt?"

Shem swung off his mount and led the horse toward the stable. "He is fine. I am sure he will be back to swinging his mallet before midday."

There was no mistaking the malice in Shem's voice.

His brothers headed for the stables in silence behind him and were met by their relieved wives before they reached it.

Zarah waited in the road, arms at her sides but hands trembling, for Noah to reach home.

Noah's horse was slow in coming, no doubt exhausted from the long day and night on the road, and Noah did not look much better. He dismounted before he reached her and led the horse until he stood before her.

"Nothing?" she asked.

He shook his head. "It is as if they never traveled along that road. No one we passed had seen them. We went far into the night and never saw them camped."

She nodded and joined him in the walk toward the stable, hugging her arms around herself in the early-morning chill. The space between them was only a breath, but it seemed like a chasm.

"Shem says they will load supplies and head back out."

Noah grunted. "I have told them they are needed here. We are so close to finishing."

"I don't think Shem agrees. Nor his brothers, perhaps."

"I know." They had reached the stable, and the three men had already put up their horses and disappeared into the house.

Zarah helped Noah feed and water his horse in silence. The weight of that silence nearly suffocated her.

They entered the house to find the three men and two wives talking of preparations. Na'el and Aris were discussing the food that needed to be cooked and packed for the journey the men would take. The three sons were arguing about the best route to Tikov.

The house smelled of porridge that had gone bad, and the fire had been left untended, its ashes already cold.

"We have been along that way and seen nothing," Ham was saying. "Why not take the road to the south entrance of the city? Perhaps someone has seen—"

"Because the north entrance is closer, and I don't want to spend one extra moment on the road, if Salbeth is in that city, with that man—" Shem broke off, ran a hand through his hair, and seemed unable to speak.

Japheth broke the tie. "We won't find them on the road by the time we get there. It's more sensible to reach the city sooner."

Noah had stood at the door since entering the house but now took a step inside.

Zarah reached out to catch his arm, to hold him back, but then let her hand drop. She had no right.

"I have spoken about this already. The building must continue, and I cannot lose all three of you."

The men turned on him as one.

"So you would have me simply abandon her?" Shem's eyes flashed. "What about your God's sacred instructions? That *you and your wife, and your sons and your sons' wives*, will enter the ship when the destruction comes? Have you forgotten those words, Father?"

Zarah sucked in a breath and bit her lip at Shem's disrespectful tone.

Her mouth felt as though it were full of the soured porridge and cold ashes.

And Noah said nothing.

Shem's face darkened. His father's refusal to answer was an answer in itself. Abandon Salbeth.

Hot, unshed tears burned at Zarah's eyes.

"It is my fault."

The words tumbled from her lips before she had a chance to catch them back.

All five turned to her, with expressions that were uncomprehending.

"Salbeth." She stuttered over the words. "What has happened. It is my fault." In the thudding heartbeats after that announcement, her body swayed where she sat on the bench. She braced her back against the wall to keep from tumbling to the ground.

"What are you saying?" Shem's eyes were dark.

"All of this is retribution. Dagon would not let me leave." She raised her eyes to them. "All those years ago. He was—obsessed—with me. But I could not be part of what he was doing any longer."

Noah sank to the bench beside her. "The rumors? They are true? Of the women being taken for some evil breeding project—"

"It is true." She could not look at them. "And now, he is taking his revenge for my leaving, by taking someone he knows is dear to me."

There was nothing more to say. And the silence said too much.

After some minutes, Noah stood. "I will offer a sacrifice."

For her sins, she knew.

She let him go, but then a few minutes later followed him outside.

The sky seemed a muddy shade of brown and the air felt sticky and close. Noah had already chosen the sacrificial goat, and the dumb animal now chewed grass beside the altar as Noah prepared the wood for the fire.

The familiar nausea that always accompanied the sacrifices hit her like a rush of hot wind across the fields. She stood back as Noah scooped up the small goat, pulled a knife from the belt around his tunic, and slit the animal's throat.

Moments later, the animal lay across the gray altar stones, stained black by the blood of countless animals before it. Noah struck a stone and the dry grass burst into a tiny flame, then spread.

Memories assaulted her once more. Memories of Dagon, standing over the altar of Sin, chanting a low and mournful dirge as he sacrificed to the moon god.

Her body felt hot now, as though it burned with the altar fire, from deep within her. Guilt and rage fueled each other and left her breathless. She clenched her fists and her fingernails bit deep into her palms.

Noah turned at last, as though he had known she was there all this time. His eyes were cold. So cold.

She approached and stood beside him, but he turned back to the altar.

Noah hated deceit. He always said that deceit was the first iniquity. The Lie told in the Garden that had expelled the First Father from Eden and kept them all searching for a way back to God ever since.

The only thing Noah hated more than deceit was the cult of Sin, to which she had willingly given herself for so long.

"Shem will have to go to Tikov."

It was a strange thing for him to say, as they stood there watching the goat burn. She said nothing.

"If Salbeth is there, in the Temple of Tikov as you say, then he must go."

Zarah nodded. "I will work in the ship, in his place."

Noah snorted, a soft sound but one filled with derision at the thought of Zarah's skills being used to build. "You have done enough."

The words were like a blow to her heart.

Noah was quiet a moment, watching the flames lick at the singed goat hair. "We will pray that we will return in time."

With that he turned and headed back to the house.

Zarah stayed at the altar, wishing that the death of the animal truly could atone for her guilt.

CHAPTER TWENTY-EIGHT

She could not bear to be near them, any of them, but where was there to go?

The fields were not safe, the city was not safe. She could hide in the ship, but they would find her there.

And so, when the family had bedded down for a restless night of waiting for dawn and the travel to Tikov, Zarah slipped from the house, ran across the moonlit back field, to the only other place she'd ever felt safe.

Grandfather's house was dark and smelled of disuse. How quickly his absence had made the place feel like the grave, instead the haven of light and love it had once been.

She curled up in the corner of his tiny home, covered herself with one of his frayed blankets, and shivered despite the warm night.

Where are you, Grandfather?

Where did men go, when they had gone to earth?

Where would all of them go—those who lived in Kish and those who lived even in Tikov—when the end came?

Methuselah's seven-day warning loomed large in her thoughts, as it surely must in the minds of the rest of the family.

Only three days left. Could Shem get Salbeth and return in time?

The blanket smelled of Grandfather. She brought it to her face, buried her tears in it and let them flow freely for the first time in days. She was so tired. Tired of the work, tired of trying to remain strong. Tired of betrayal and failure. Of the criticism of her children and the displeasure of her husband.

Again, she wondered why any of it mattered anymore. Why did the One God not simply wipe them *all* from the earth and start again with a new Eden, a new race that would not choose to disobey?

A sound outside the doorway straightened her spine where she sat in the corner.

An animal? One of the many creatures that had never been seen before they started trekking across their fields toward the ship?

But no, this was no animal, lifting the latch of the door and sliding it open against the worn dirt floor.

"Zarah?"

Na'el.

Zarah sighed, the sound still muffled by Grandfather's blanket.

"I am here."

Na'el's shuffling steps drew closer. Her thin frame was outlined by the moonlight in the doorway.

She put out her hands as if searching. "What are you doing? I was on the roof—I couldn't sleep. I saw you cross the field."

"Nothing. Just wanted to think. Alone."

Na'el drew herself up and folded her arms.

Even in the sliver of moonlight, Zarah could sense her annoyance.

"Well, I suppose I didn't need to worry then, did I?"

Zarah closed her eyes. She was too tired for Na'el as well.

"You don't need to worry about me, daughter."

But Na'el wasn't finished. "It seems like someone should! Every time we get close to being finished with this—this—project—you do something to make it more difficult."

"Why are you here, Na'el? What do you want?"

"I told you, I was worried."

"If you are so worried about me, why do you continue to plague me with your sharp words?"

"Sharp *words*? You are offended by words? When your actions are about to send my husband toward the point of a temple guard's spear? How dare you speak to me of words!"

Ah, here was the reason she had crossed the dark field.

Zarah climbed to her feet, fatigued and a bit unsteady.

"If Ham goes with Shem, he will be safe, Na'el. The One God has said—"

"How can I know what your God has said? He does not speak to me!"

Zarah smiled sadly in the dark. How often had she said that very thing?

"And if Ham dies, what then? No man in this city will take me for a wife, if Noah's destruction does not come. And if it does, what then? I will be alone! Alone and unloved and childless!"

A quick response came to Zarah but died on her lips. Again, how much like herself Na'el sounded. Afraid of being unloved and alone. No child to give her meaning, worried she would be useless.

Was this the fear that gnawed at Na'el and made her surly and difficult?

The very same fear that drove Zarah to try to solve every problem, right every wrong?

She reached across the darkened room with a surge of compassion. "Na'el, you will not—"

But the girl pulled back from her touch, spun, and fled the house.

Zarah was too tired to chase her.

She returned to her corner and Grandfather's blanket and sank to the floor once more.

What was it that he had told her, right here as he lay dying? She struggled already to remember the words.

You try so hard, do so much, to make them love you. To make them see you. But the One God loves and sees you. And that is enough.

Was it true?

Perhaps it was time to believe it.

If the One God loved her, if He *saw* her, then nothing else mattered. Not the opinions of her family. Not Etana or the townspeople. Not even the obsessive wrath of Dagon.

She needed only to fall into that grace, into that mercy, and trust it.

She buried her face once more in Grandfather's blanket.

Yes. Yes, she would place herself there, in the way of God's mercy and grace.

And then I will go before you, child. Rather than watch you run ahead of Me.

She lifted her head, turned it to the left and right.

The words had come...but from where? Spoken aloud or perhaps only in her mind but as distinctly as if someone sat beside her speaking as a friend.

"Who is there?"

She whispered the question, already knowing the answer and perhaps fearing it as well.

I am.

A chill ran across her shoulders, and her throat went dry.

"What do you want me to do?"

The question seemed to make sense, but were the words misplaced?

Follow.

When the Voice had come to Noah, it had given such detail, such specifics of this great ship they were to build. Was she only to get this one word? Follow whom? Follow where?

"Where do you want me to go?"

Follow.

She exhaled, trying to hold on to the Voice, begging with the unspoken desire of her heart to hear more. More. *Please.*

You long for purpose. I have ordained that you will be the mother of all who come after you.

She sucked in a breath.

But you must be willing to fight.

She had never been willing to fight. Had always sought peace. Worked to erase conflict.

"Fight how? Where?"

Follow.

She waited, hoping for more.

The night stretched on, but the Voice was silent.

She slept, curled up on the floor and dreaming of better days, when Grandfather had played with her three boys in the grasses, when Noah and she had farmed the land side by side, when the sun shone down on them and they pushed away the growing evil in the city.

And then she dreamed of future days. When she herself would play with her own grandchildren in the grasses. When Noah and she would once again grow food under the sun, after the world had been washed clean.

When she awoke, the sun had risen.

She stretched against cramped limbs and pushed the hair back from her throbbing temples. She was getting too old to sleep in the cold.

The men would be getting ready to leave for Tikov. She should help pack their provisions and see them off.

She crossed the field back to the main house slowly. What had it all meant, the words she heard last night?

It was impossible to say, yet for some reason she felt as though a dark burden had been lifted.

Only three days remained now. It was time for the One God to do the impossible.

CHAPTER TWENTY-NINE

Noah awoke the next morning disoriented and groggy. He rubbed his face and eyes, rolled to one side, and focused his gaze on Zarah's empty sleeping mat. Was she awake so early?

It was not surprising that Zarah had fled the house after his rough words with her beside the altar. He had been unkind. He owed her an apology. Her revelation of her past, of the years before he had known her, had been such a surprise, and had shaken everything he believed about her. But still, he should not have been unkind.

He stumbled to the main gathering room of the house, but it was empty. The courtyard and rooftop as well. His sons must still be in their beds, and their wives with them.

At the thought of the women, guilt stabbed at him. Shem did not have Salbeth at his side. And Noah had tried to do all he could to convince Shem to leave it that way. That could not be, he could see that now. But Ham and Japheth, they must stay and help with the ark.

The sun was barely up, but he crossed the field to the project that had consumed so many years now. The ark cast a long shadow across the fields. The shadow seemed to swallow the

fallow ground and sparse stalks of grain that had grown without sowing or reaping this year.

Inside, in the gloom, he crossed to one of the many pens
he had built in the lowest deck and braced his hands against
the rail around it. The animals were quiet for now, but the
smell of them all combined with the smell of the bitumen tar
was too strong down here. It made his head ache.

He climbed the ramps to breathe the morning air, though
it was nearly as heavy. The air had been strange lately. One
more oddity that made him certain the end was near.

Noah tilted his head. The morning was so silent. No birds
twittered the coming of the day. No insects. Only silence. The
hair on the back of his neck prickled.

A shuffling sound behind him turned him round.

"Father."

He nodded to Shem, standing at the top of the steps. "Did
you rest?"

"We leave soon."

Noah turned away, ran his hand over the rough wood of
the roof's rim. Everywhere he looked, there was evidence of
breakage, of half-finished details, and of ill-fitting joints.
His father would have crafted this ark to perfection, even if
the time were short. Lamech was a master with wood.

Why, God? Why me and not my father?

It was a question with no answer. He was so much more
likely to fail at shipbuilding, just as he had failed to turn his
neighbors back to God.

"I know you must go, Shem. I cannot ask you to stay. But your brothers. They must continue the work with me."

"You are obsessed with this work, Father. You let it consume you. Let it become more important than anything else. More than your family."

"Do not speak to me of family!" Noah kicked at the ark's hull.

Shem kicked twice at a bench beside him, as if to go one better than his father. "Give your command to my brothers yourself. I will not tell them to abandon my wife."

He disappeared down the steps, and a moment later was crossing the fields beneath the ark.

Noah stayed, speaking his prayer into the morning sky and then listening until finally he knew what must be done.

CHAPTER THIRTY

The men were already packed and saying their goodbyes by the time Zarah reached the house.

She entered without speaking and received barely a glance from the two women, who were crying softly over the departure of their husbands.

Shem tied a pouch under his outer tunic and then secured it with a band. Probably some dried fish or fruit, but perhaps a bit of silver as well, if there was any to be had.

Noah crossed the front room of the house, put his hands on her shoulders, and looked into her eyes. "Are you well? Na'el told me you spent the night at the Grandfather's house."

She smiled up at him. "I am well."

His forehead creased in a question. "What has happened? You seem—different."

She half shrugged and leaned toward him. "Perhaps the One God also speaks to women after all."

His eyes widened, and he opened his mouth to question her further.

Shem interrupted. "We should be off."

Aris was clutching at Japheth. "What will you do? You cannot fight against an entire city. And you don't even know where Salbeth is!"

Noah held up a hand. "We have someone who can help us find our way." He turned to Zarah. "If she will."

Zarah's heart thudded. "What are you saying?"

He took her hands in his. "I have not been as understanding a husband as I should have been, perhaps. But I know that you might be the only one who can help us find Salbeth and get her back. I am asking you to trust me. I am asking you to follow me."

Follow.

She couldn't speak.

The eyes of her sons and the two wives were on her, waiting for her response.

She nodded, tears welling. "I will follow you, Husband. Yes, I will follow you."

It took only a few additional minutes to prepare a satchel for herself, mount Hazir behind Noah, and wave to Aris and Na'el, who promised to care for the animals and finish preparations inside the ship. Na'el even said she'd finish coating the inside of the port cistern with pitch.

And then they were off, riding back over the same roads she'd foolishly traveled alone just last week. This time they would make it all the way to Tikov.

They rode hard, farther into the night than was probably safe, made a hasty camp along the side of the road, and were back on horseback before the sun had fully risen.

Before long, the dusty outlines of Tikov began to scratch at the pale sky above the horizon ahead. They passed a few travelers, heading toward Kish no doubt to trade, but otherwise the journey had been thankfully uneventful.

Noah led the way, with Zarah clutching from behind, as they approached the city's gates, built clumsily into the rough wall that surrounded Tikov. The heavy gates stood open at this hour, with beggars squatting just inside, hoping to prevail upon the generosity of newcomers who had not yet spent their silver within the city.

Zarah stared at an old beggar as they passed.

He looked up into her face, and his own was covered with sores. A fly landed on his forehead, and he didn't move to swat it away.

It had been so long, and yet she could have described Tikov as though she'd seen it yesterday. More crowded, perhaps, but the same large well in the round clearing not far through the gates. The same mud-brick houses crowded up close, built higher and wider than those in Kish, as though the city had something to prove over its lesser counterparts.

The four horses with their riders picked their way carefully through the teeming street. Children, donkeys, and carts joined the market vendors and shoppers, fighting for the right of way. All of them talking, yelling, arguing.

She resisted the urge to cover her ears. It was not the level of noise as much as the chaos. So different from their quiet home at the edge of Kish, amid their fields. But being in the midst of it brought back the years of living in Tikov as though she'd never been gone, and if she put her fists to her ears it would only be in hopes of drowning out the memories along with the noise.

Noah half turned his head toward her. "Which way to the temple?"

Despite her position, just behind him on the horse, she still needed to lean forward to make sure she was heard. "Down that way"—she pointed straight ahead—"toward the very center of the city."

He nodded, then motioned to their sons to follow him to the left. They needed time to prepare before breaching the temple.

"Stop!" A skinny man, tall and gangly, ran toward them, yelling.

Zarah's fingers tightened on Noah's tunic. She had expected more time before being recognized or accosted.

But the angry man twisted into the crowd to the right, shaking his fist. "Stop, you filthy little beggar!"

Ahead of him, a child no higher than her elbow darted through the throng, clutching some ill-gotten gain in his fist and avoiding his angry pursuer.

He was indeed filthy, as were so many of the people in this city. Was there no water for washing? Or did they simply not care?

They passed a row of squat houses, with a group of quarreling women outside. Two of them were grabbing at something—clothing, perhaps—tugging it between them as if they both owned it and screaming at each other.

Zarah rested her forehead against Noah's shoulder and wrapped her arms more tightly around his waist. Tikov was a roiling mess of angry, dirty, miserable people.

This was what a city dedicated to the moon god had become? Did they not see that their worship was fruitless, that it brought no peace, no joy?

A quiet alley between houses at last presented itself, and Shem led their horses into the shadows. They all dismounted and grouped quietly, with the horses shielding them from prying eyes in the street.

"Tell us again, Mother," Ham said. "Now that we are here, explain again the layout of the temple and how we get to the lower level where Salbeth is likely to be found."

Shem's face was set like stone. "And how many guards I will need to kill to get my wife."

"Shem!" Noah grabbed his son's shoulder. "Pray that no one will die by your hand today!"

"So that they may all die in a few days, when the end comes?" Shem's voice was cutting, his look piercing.

"Yes. If that is the will of God. Then, yes."

Shem lowered his eyes at the deep sorrow in Noah's voice.

Zarah touched Noah's elbow, though it would offer little comfort, she knew.

"I will tell you again." She paused. "But I will tell you how to get there when the guards are otherwise occupied. With me."

Noah scowled. "What are you talking about?"

"Dagon was clear. He wants me to give myself up to him, in place of Salbeth."

"Mother!" Japheth and Ham cried her name in unison.

Shem and Noah chimed in with "No!" at the same time.

She smiled at their outrage and held up her palms to stem their objections. "Hear me out." She took a deep breath. She had to explain this carefully, or they would never let her do it. "I have no intention of giving myself back to Dagon. But neither do I intend to let my husband and sons walk into certain death. No, Shem, do not interrupt. You must trust me when I tell you that Dagon has guards at every entrance, and they will cut you down before you ever reach Salbeth."

Shem was pacing now, pacing and shaking his head.

Her heart welled with pity. He loved his wife and must be going mad thinking of her in that temple with Dagon.

"The only chance you will have is if I approach from the west side entrance, the smaller entrance that only ever had two guards, and if I announce myself and make sure that it takes both of them to escort me to Dagon."

"And how are you going to ensure that?" Noah's face had gone an angry shade of red.

She smiled. "Trust me. I know how to cause a problem."

Her husband was not amused. "There is no way I am going to let you hand yourself over to that evil man."

"I will be a distraction only. I will keep him busy, and those guards, for enough time for the four of you to get in behind me, descend to the lower level where he keeps the animal pens—and sometimes women—and get Salbeth out." She passed over that bit about the women as quickly as she could.

Despite her effort, Shem exploded in rage. "My wife is penned like an animal?"

"Shh," she touched his arm and glanced toward the street. "Not for long, not for long."

Noah was looking toward the street as well. "Do I dare ask why the high priest keeps women in pens?"

"That is an explanation for another day. Today, we get Salbeth." And yet even as she said it, she knew there were not many days left. Not for Tikov. Not for the world.

Shem was nodding and mounting his horse. "Today we get Salbeth."

CHAPTER THIRTY-ONE

Zarah would have followed Shem on his horse from the alley immediately, but Noah held her back.

Apparently he was not finished with the conversation.

"And once we get Salbeth out of there," he said, "do you expect Dagon to simply let you walk away and return home with us?"

Shem turned his horse's head back toward his family. "Mother, I was not thinking—"

She smiled and patted his leg. "I will find a way out of there."

Noah was still holding her arm. "Not good enough."

She sighed. "I know Dagon, and I know that place. If I cannot convince him to let me leave willingly, I will escape on my own as soon as I am out of his sight."

The four men did not appear convinced.

"I will meet you back here, in this alley, before nightfall. If I do not come…"

"If you do not come, then we will storm that vile temple and do whatever we must to get you out!"

Shem's anger sounded as fierce for her as it did for Salbeth, and it warmed Zarah to hear it.

"This is madness!" Noah was pacing in the narrow alley. "I cannot allow you—"

"It is done, husband."

She spoke the words confidently. Unlike her earlier attempts to do whatever she could to solve her family's problems, her heart told her that the One God had asked her to follow her family here to this place, and He would protect her.

And so she kissed each of them, wrapped a head covering over her hair, and whispered final words to Noah as she embraced him. "Get them back to safety, whatever happens." She gave him a look that said everything. With or without her, he must return their family to the ship. Their sons and their wives— they were the hope for the future.

She left them in the alley and walked toward the temple alone.

They would follow at a distance, keeping her in sight, waiting for the opening she would give them at the western entrance of the temple.

How many times, as a younger woman, had she walked this road? Coming back from the market, from the well, from time spent wandering the city alone simply to be free of that place?

And yet it was none of those times that nipped at her memory today. It was only the first time. When she was much smaller. Her tiny hand gripped painfully by her father. Wondering why they went to the temple alone, with nothing to offer.

She bumped along through the crowded street, barely noticing those who jostled and shoved. She pushed forward until the temple was in sight, and then she slowed.

Despite the childhood memories that surged, the temple was larger than she remembered. Its tan stone walls, carved with strange deities that were part human, part beast, stood as high as four men. A wall made of mud bricks had been constructed around the courtyard in front since she had been here last. Perhaps the act of a suspicious high priest who was hated as much as he was feared.

Would there still be a west entrance? Some sort of gate there for her to walk through?

She risked a glance backward, but the four men were keeping well hidden and she saw no one she knew.

She began a slow circle around the wall, her fingers trailing along the rough bricks.

Was anyone watching her strange procession? Wondering why she did not enter through the front gate?

There! A gap in the stones ahead. So there was a way to reach the west entrance. She tried not to hurry her steps. Give the men time to get in position.

There were no guards at the opening in the wall itself, but standing at its edge she saw the expected two at the narrow temple door. So the wall existed only as a deterrent and a way to defend against a mob attack on the temple. Perhaps the moon god was not as revered as he had been when she lived in this place.

Zarah lifted her head, squared her shoulders, and stepped through the wall.

The attention of both guards flicked toward her, then away, as if bored by the sight of her. They were young. Too young to remember her.

She walked slowly, wanting to preserve the surprise of her plan.

When she was not much more than an arm's length away from the door, she clutched at her tunic, studied the ground, and began to wail. Softly at first, then letting the sound build in her chest, rising louder and louder as she swayed on her feet.

She dared not look at the guards, but certainly she had their attention.

"Get out of here, woman. Go home to your husband if you wish to cry!"

Yes, she had their attention.

She let out another keening wail. "My husband is dead! Dead! After I made sacrifices and prayers and gave all I had to the high priest and to Sin!"

She reached down and grabbed up handfuls of dirt from the ground. They would be expecting her to rain the dirt down on her own head in sorrow.

Instead she threw a handful into each of their faces.

They both yelled in outrage and scrabbled at their eyes.

Zarah darted between them, into the temple.

She didn't expect to outrun them. But she would get them as far from that entrance as possible.

They were still yelling and sputtering behind her, but she could hear the heavy slap of sandals on the flagstones laid in the temple floor.

She ran as fast as her legs would take her, tunic pulled up above her knees, breath huffing in her chest, toward the central courtyard of the temple.

A little farther. Just a bit farther.

And then their hands were on her arms, rough and unforgiving, and she was yanked backward off her feet.

She screamed and thrashed. It was only an act. She had little real fear of these two boys. Not when Salbeth's very life was in danger. But she needed to keep these two here, with her, and that door unguarded for as long as she could.

"Let me go! I want to see the high priest!"

"Oh, you will see him, old woman!"

The guard gripping her right arm got his face down against hers.

It was still flecked with dirt, even in his eyelashes.

They dragged her forward toward the altar and shoved her to her knees.

She could not let them leave her here and take the risk they would return to their posts. She grabbed at the ankles of the guard nearest her and tried to pull him off his feet.

"Take me to the high priest!"

"No need." A smooth voice carried across the courtyard, so much like four nights ago in Kish that Zarah felt disoriented, as though everything in her past were happening again.

The two guards hauled her to her feet.

She kept her head down for a few moments longer, still trying to give the men time.

"What have we here?"

Dagon's feet slid across the flagstones, inching closer.

One of the guards shoved her forward. "She was screaming about her dead husband."

With her head still down, she saw only the lower half of Dagon's tunic as he appeared in front of her.

He lifted her chin, looked into her eyes, and smiled.

"Is this true, Zarah? Is your shipbuilding husband dead?"

She had not thought about this part of her plan. How to keep him occupied with her, what she would say.

So she said nothing. Instead, she closed her eyes and took in the sounds and the smells of this place she hated so much.

The altar behind Dagon reeked of blood and incense. From somewhere in the inner recesses of the temple came the singsong chant of priestesses, such as the young girls that were once under her command.

She opened her eyes and took in the courtyard. It was devoid of all decoration, except for the stone altar and a few stone statues of beasts like the ones carved into the outside walls of the temple, and a plain stone bench on the other side of the altar. The late-day sun slanted across the flagstones like a trail of yellow.

"Leave us," Dagon said to the two guards.

Zarah's throat was on fire. Was it enough time?

"You are the one who should be dead, Dagon!" She threw herself at him and pounded his chest with her fists.

As she hoped, the two guards yanked her backward again.

Dagon laughed. "Go," he said again. "I can handle the little priestess."

"Do not call me that!"

The guards were retreating.

She could think of nothing more to call them back. She prayed her men were beneath the temple by now and that they had found Salbeth.

"But that is what you are, and what you will always be, my dear Zarah. Or did you think that Sin forgot you?"

"I care nothing for your demons. I serve the true God, the One God."

He shrugged. "Then what are you doing here?"

She did not want to suggest that he free Salbeth, as he had promised. She doubted he would do it, but she could not take the chance of him sending for the girl. Not yet.

"You said you would leave my husband alone, let him keep his ship, if I came."

"Ah." Dagon ran a finger down her jawline. "So all of this is for him. For your mad husband. I am saddened."

"Did you think I would *want* to return here? After everything?"

"Come, sit with me, Zarah."

He glided to the stone bench across from them and sat.

She must keep him occupied, so she joined him on the bench.

"Do you remember the time we spent together, here in this courtyard, doing the work of the gods?"

"I remember everything."

He smiled. "And yet here you are."

"As I said—"

"Yes, as you said. For your husband. Why is it that I don't believe you?"

"I don't care what you believe."

The courtyard fell into sudden shadow as the last of the sun's rays fell beneath the edge of the temple's outer wall. A chill swept Zarah's body, and she shivered.

Dagon was still smiling. He touched her thigh with his fingertips. "Shall we light the fires for warmth?"

"Tell me what you want with me."

Dagon stood and paced in front of her. "I want the truth, my dear Zarah. You come to offer yourself to me, in exchange for your husband's ship. And yet you say nothing of the girl. Am I to believe you do not care what happens to her?"

Zarah shrugged, but her heartbeat sped up. "You will leave my family alone. The girl also, of course."

"Hmm. Of course." He circled the altar and placed his hands on it, facing her. "I remember everything as well, Zarah. How you came to me, so young and innocent. How you helped me to build our following, to strengthen the city's worship of Sin. How you helped me with our...project."

"Do not speak of it."

"Yes, there it is. The anger." He leaned forward. "I remember how you betrayed me, Zarah. I remember."

"So you want to kill me? Is that what you want?"

"Guards!"

His sudden shout toward the temple entrance startled her. She gripped the edges of the stone bench beneath her with chilled fingers.

Two men came at once, different from the younger ones who had been at the west entrance.

Dagon motioned with his head. "Bring the girl. The new one."

They disappeared at once.

So this was the moment. What would Dagon do, if her men had been successful in freeing Salbeth?

"Let us see what your daughter thinks of the way her mother used to serve here in this temple."

"She is not my daughter."

He frowned, lips parted.

She had succeeded in surprising him. "She is the wife of my son."

"Hmm. She is so much like you. Strange. The moment I saw her with you in Kish, I was taken back to the days before your betrayal…"

He seemed lost in reminiscing, and she did not interrupt.

The air grew more chilled. How long until nightfall, when she had promised to meet Noah and her sons in the alley? Did she really believe she could free herself from this madman?

Dagon seemed to grow tired of waiting. "Guards!"

When no one came, he yelled again. This time, the two younger she'd already met came at his summons.

"Where are the other two? I sent them for the new girl."

When the two looked confused, Dagon waved them out. "Go, get the girl. And tell the others they had better present themselves as well!"

The singing in the back of the temple stopped. Zarah felt as though time itself had stopped.

The two guards returned a few moments later.

"She is gone." The taller one, whose ankles she had grabbed, looked terrified.

Dagon whirled to face them. "Gone? Where are the guards?"

"One dead. One badly injured."

Dagon spun back to face her, a slow smile that was evil itself spreading across his face.

"Ah, Zarah. So you betray me once again."

CHAPTER THIRTY-TWO

Noah watched Zarah enter the western side of the temple enclosure with a hollow feeling in the pit of his stomach. This was a mistake.

Their confrontation with the high priest back in Kish had left no doubt as to the kind of man he was. Even if he had done no actual violence in that little temple or in the fields in front of their ship, it was clear that he was borne of evil and served evil with his whole being.

How could Noah have let Zarah walk into that place?

He and his sons had tied their horses to the wheel of an abandoned broken cart in the street, given a bit of silver to a young boy to keep watch, and crept as close as they dared to the temple wall. And all the time Noah had been chastising himself for letting her go.

And then he heard her screaming.

He started forward, fear surging into his chest.

Ham grabbed Noah's shoulder and shook his head.

Yes, yes, Zarah was yelling about her dead husband. Well, he was not dead yet.

Shem edged closer to the gap in the stone wall and peered around the edge for only a moment. He raised his arm to hold back the others and then looked again.

"Come, they are taking her inside!"

The four rounded the gap into the enclosure, then ran to the temple's exterior wall and flattened themselves against it.

Again, Shem edged to the doorway and looked inside, then motioned for the other three to follow.

Inside, to the left as Zarah had described, into a dark corridor that ran the length of this side of the temple.

Noah followed his sons, glanced back over his shoulder. They had not been followed yet. He felt at his waist for the blade secreted there and prayed he would not have to use it.

A narrow door at the end of the corridor appeared in the gloom, just as Zarah had said it would. Shem disappeared into the dark rectangle of empty space, with Ham and Japheth close behind.

One last look behind him, and Noah dove into the darkness with them.

Down, down a packed-earth ramp. Ahead, a bit of torchlight flickered.

They rounded a corner, each in turn, and when Noah followed last he nearly ran into Japheth's back.

At the sight in front of him, Noah exhaled the breath he had been holding and whispered a curse against Sin and his followers.

Zarah had said these pens were for animals, and the underground dungeon certainly smelled like animal pens, but all Noah could see in the stalls that lined the earthen walls were women. Dozens of women. Sitting, lying in the straw, some tied up and others too weak to escape.

Shem was already moving down the center of the pens, quietly calling Salbeth's name.

"Shem!" She was there, toward the end of the low-ceilinged room, reaching for her husband.

Japheth was moving too but not toward Salbeth. He was kicking down wooden posts and hacking ropes that bound other women.

"What are you doing?" Ham's voice was too loud.

Japheth didn't look up from his work. "We can't leave them here!"

Ham looked to Noah for support, his eyes angry. "What difference does it make? You are going to get us all killed!"

Japheth ignored his brother.

Shem was soon pushing Salbeth toward Noah. "Take her and go, Father. We will join you soon!"

Salbeth clutched at Noah, and he circled her waist with his arm to give her support.

Ham was right. If the end of all things was truly upon them, and if only he and his family were to be saved, then it made little difference whether these women were freed today or not.

And yet what kind of people would the One God be saving, if they left them here in this pit?

With four of them working, it took only a few minutes to cut all the ropes that kept the women prisoner.

"Come," Noah said, lifting Salbeth from where she had collapsed to the ground. "We have done all we can. We must go."

They headed for the upward-slanting ramp, Noah and Shem supporting Salbeth between them.

Just before they reached the bottom and began the ascent, two figures appeared above them, one holding a torch.

Guards.

They were four against two, but they must make quiet work of it or more guards would be upon them in moments.

Ham and Japheth charged upward, silent and swift, with blades drawn.

The guards were not expecting an attack.

Noah pushed Salbeth into Shem's arms and rushed to join his sons at the top of the ramp.

Ham grabbed the torch from the surprised man's grip and used it like a club against the side of the guard's head.

Japheth had already barreled into the other man and the two were locked together, both grunting.

It was over by the time Noah could have helped. Two guards on the ground, one of them probably only unconscious after Ham's blow to his head, but Japheth stood over the other man, his eyes wide.

And then he vomited.

He still held the knife, now bloody.

A moment later Shem was hurrying past them, nearly carrying Salbeth now.

Noah grabbed Japheth's arm.

His son did not move.

"Come, come, Japheth."

Ham joined Shem and his wife at the edge of the door.

"Japheth, we must go!"

Other women were scrambling up the ramp behind them now, eager to escape.

The commotion behind them seemed to wake Japheth from his stupor. He stumbled forward, grabbed Noah's arm, righted himself, and followed his brothers.

They moved with stealth back down the corridor, toward the entrance they had come through. Noah prayed that Zarah was somehow both keeping Dagon from discovering them and at the same time already far from this wicked place. He felt the bile surge in his own throat and forced himself to keep moving.

Out, out through the temple door, through the stone wall enclosure, out into the street.

They did not stop moving, and no guards shouted or gave chase behind them.

The women they had freed were just as silent, spilling into the street and then scattering in all directions.

They untied their horses with haste.

"Come," Noah said, "walk quickly, heads down."

They led their beasts down the street, away from the temple, without mounting so as not to draw attention. Shem kept Salbeth between himself and his horse, and the girl placed a steadying hand on the horse's flank as they hurried toward the far side of the city.

They neared the alley where they had agreed to meet Zarah.

Noah ran ahead, pulling Hazir and still praying she would be there.

The alley was empty.

The others filed in, blocked the view from the street with their horses once again, and finally gave their full attention to Salbeth.

"Were you hurt? What did they do to you?" Shem was holding her at arm's length, looking her up and down.

She shook her head. "The journey here was rough. But the worst they did was give me no food and water."

She looked half-starved already, the poor thing. Noah grabbed his waterskin from the pouch slung across Hazir and held it to her lips.

She drank greedily, then put her head back against Shem's shoulder. "I knew you would come. I knew you would."

A shout in the street drew their attention, and Salbeth clutched at Shem's arm.

Ham peered beyond the horses. "It is nothing—not about us."

"Please," Salbeth said. "Let us leave. Go home. Now."

Noah raked a hand through his hair. "I wish we could. But Zarah is still in there."

Salbeth's lips parted. "Zarah? They took her too?"

"She went in to cause a distraction while we rescued you."

The girl's shoulders sagged. "Oh, Mother." She bit her lip and tears slipped from the corners of her eyes.

Japheth was still silent. Staring at the ground.

Noah touched his arm. "Son?"

"I killed a man." Still looking at the ground, Japheth's words were barely audible.

Noah pulled his son to his chest. "You had no choice."

He felt his son stiffen in his arms and pulled away. There was blood on his tunic. He reached for Japheth's hand. "You are hurt!"

Japheth turned his hand over, palm upward. "The knife— it slipped."

The gash across the heel of his hand was deep.

Noah ripped the edge off the bottom of his tunic and wrapped Japheth's palm. "We must get Zarah now, get out of here." He finished the bandage and moved toward his horse.

Ham folded arms across his chest, blocking Noah's path. "If we go back in there, we cannot leave Salbeth alone, and Japheth will be of little use with that injured hand. We barely made it out with only two guards against us. Do you think so few of us can breach all the guards of Tikov?"

"We must try!" Noah fought to keep his voice under control.

"Father, Ham is right. We cannot force our way in there now, when they have surely discovered the women missing and the guards we attacked. They will know that we will come after Mother. They will be waiting for us."

"Then what do you suggest? That we leave your mother there?"

He waited for an answer, but his sons were silent.

CHAPTER THIRTY-THREE

Zarah had expected to be locked up in the dungeon below the temple.

When Dagon led her to one of the most luxurious rooms in the back of the building, she raised her eyebrows but said nothing.

He clucked his tongue at her. "What must you think of me, Zarah, to believe I would mistreat you? No, of course you will have nothing but the finest. All will be as it once was." He swept an arm toward the interior of the room, which was cool and dimly lit only by a small window, high in the wall, lit by the dusk.

The room itself was hung with beautiful fabrics, and the floor covered in an abundance of soft bedding. A carved marble bench hugged the wall, and a floral scent wafted across her senses.

Did he expect her to thank him?

"Rest here for a time, my dear. I will send for you when the evening meal is prepared. We will dine together."

He bowed himself out of the room, as if he were nothing more than a gracious host.

Zarah crossed the room to the small window and ran her hand along the silky fabric hung there. Would the bench be high enough for her to reach the window and climb out? But no, the window was too small. She would never fit. Dagon would have thought of that.

She returned to the doorway. Perhaps Dagon would not expect her to slip away so quickly.

Two guards stood at either side.

How had he placed them there already?

So, she was a prisoner, even if she was not in a dungeon.

Exhaustion suddenly seized her, and she sank to the bedding, sitting with her back braced against the wall. She would have preferred to have resisted anything Dagon offered, but the temptation to rest was too strong.

Where were Noah and her sons now? She looked to the window, as if she could see into the street. Did they have Salbeth? The report of the injured guards would seem to suggest it.

Through the window, the first stars glimmered in the darkening sky.

I will meet you in the alley before nightfall.

What would Noah do when she did not return?

Please, Noah, give me more time. It was too dangerous for him to storm into this place with only her sons for an army.

Would he trust her to find a way out?

The fabric was too soft and her eyes too heavy. She would need rest for whatever was ahead. Just a few minutes to lie down, to close her eyes…

She dreamed of another time. Of her first day in the Temple of Tikov.

Curled up in the darkness in a tiny room shared with several other young women. They had been unkind to the newcomer, and her confusion over the departure of her father had cowed her into submission to whatever they told her to do.

Why had he left her? Why did he return to her mother and her sisters but decide that she was not worthy to bring home again?

The exchange of silver between the high priest and her father had not gone unnoticed. She was worth more as a thing to be sold than she was as a person.

In her dreams, her father was laughing. Laughing at the way the other priestesses mistreated her. Laughing at the years spent growing into a woman, understanding her place here, doing what she needed to do to survive.

She awoke to complete darkness.

Had Dagon forgotten to give her food? Had he let her wait in darkness to try to break her spirit?

Perhaps it was working.

She propped herself up, still groggy. The dream had left her cold on the inside. She felt an emptiness there, as though something important were draining out of her. What was it? She tried to reach out for it, to remember.

Truth.

It was truth that was draining out of her, being replaced by lies. The lies of the dream, the lies of the enemy.

And only the truth could fight a lie.

She sucked in a breath, whispered a prayer, and then stood.

As though Dagon had sensed the appointed time had come, he was suddenly at the doorway, a small torch in his hand.

"Zarah, forgive me. I have left you too long. Come, you must be hungry."

Her stomach rumbled in response to his question, and she wrapped her arms around her waist.

He was disappearing beyond the door.

She followed him, eyes taking in the guards still at the door, who did not follow.

He led her through the corridor that lay alongside the central courtyard, toward the back of the temple.

Where were they going? Nothing had been behind these rooms at the back when she lived here.

"We have expanded, as you can see." Dagon glanced back to make sure she was following. "The people of Tikov, and the surrounding cities, have been quite generous in their offerings to Sin."

They emerged from the back rooms into yet another open courtyard, this one much more well appointed with small pools and greenery, and a low table spread with food in the center. Torches lined the perimeter and cast a golden glow on the garden.

A private courtyard. Zarah doubted whether those who gave so generously to Sin ever made it back to this area, to see what their gifts and offerings had purchased. No, this was a luxury for the high priest alone, and for those he deemed his "favorites."

Was she truly in that position again?

Dagon extended his hand to invite her to sit at the table.

She lowered herself to a mat. Despite wishing she could refuse, she needed to eat. Whatever lay ahead, she had a feeling she would need physical strength to accomplish it.

The table was spread with roasted duck, apples, and bread spread with honey. She took a tentative bite of a piece of duck, then hungrily ate the remainder.

Always, she had one ear to the front of the temple, half waiting for the arrival of her family, and half praying that they would not come.

But the longer they lingered over the meal, with Dagon filling her mind with talk of the years that had intervened, the colder her heart grew and the more difficult it became to believe that Noah and her sons still waited somewhere, still wanted to rescue her.

Perhaps Noah had taken her final words to him to heart and had decided to return to the ship without her. She could not blame him if he had. The One God had given them only a little more time, and Noah could not disobey by wasting time in Tikov trying to rescue her.

"And that is why it is so delightful that you have returned," Dagon was saying. He paused and frowned. "Zarah, I feel as though your body has returned but your mind has not. I will need for you to listen to me."

She stifled a laugh. Odd, at such a time, that she felt like laughing. But the idea that Dagon expected her to care about his thoughts, or that she would give him any part of her attention, was too ludicrous.

"You think this is amusing? That *I* am amusing, do you?" His eyes blazed.

"I am here, Dagon. That is what you demanded, and what you have received."

A noncommittal answer, but she would not speak lies to please him.

"Hmm. Indeed." He cocked his head and placed a thin finger against his chin. "Yes, yes, I think I will."

She said nothing. It had always been like this. Dagon carried on conversations within himself that he did not share with others.

"Stay, Zarah. I have a gift for you."

She ate more of the roasted duck and apples while he was gone. It was delicious, better than anything she'd tasted in years, and she felt a bit guilty enjoying it.

But if she were to be left here until the world ended, she may as well enjoy the food.

Dagon returned, clutching something to his chest and smiling. "This will be a surprise, I have no doubt." He extended his hand and opened his palm. "Do you remember it?"

A delicate necklace lay in his palm. Six red rubies, worked into silver.

Yes, she remembered it. Could still feel the coldness of the stones against her throat as he fastened it there for the first time, when she was just becoming a woman.

She swallowed the last bite of apple and felt it slide down her throat like dust and fill her belly like rocks.

"Well? Do you remember? I have kept it all these years. Kept it for you."

He circled the table as if he would place it on her neck once more.

She gripped the edge of the table.

Zarah could not be here. Not again.

She could not be his priestess, his pet.

The One God had told her, when He spoke through the Grandfather and then again to her alone, that she was loved. Accepted. Significant. That she had a purpose.

Like the jewels she had worked into beauty all her life, she may have come from the earth and she may have been muddied over the years, but she was still valuable. Still...*wanted*.

She took up the goblet of heated wine, stood, and turned.

Dagon was smiling.

Back in the room where he had imprisoned her, she had tried to think of a plan of escape.

But here in this moment, it seemed so clear. So simple.

Run.

Had the word come from her own mind, or was it the Voice she had grown to love?

Zarah threw the heated wine into Dagon's eyes, and she ran.

CHAPTER THIRTY-FOUR

Zarah felt as though her feet had wings.

Through the back rooms of the temple, down the corridor alongside the central courtyard, through the main temple chamber, she ran like a child.

But not a frightened child.

Something had shifted inside her. Some assurance of who she was, of the One she belonged to, had bloomed in her heart. And there was no more room there for fear.

And so she ran, through the front doors of the temple into the night, down the path toward the outer stone wall, and then into the street.

If Dagon followed her, she did not hear him.

Was he still wiping the stinging wine from his eyes? Was he shrieking for guards to follow her?

She did not know, and she did not care.

The alley. Which way to the alley where she had promised to meet them?

She slowed in the street, disoriented by the darkness.

The city was still crowded and noisy. Unlike Kish, where most people were afraid to be about at night, this city carried on with drunkenness and carousing even after the sun had disappeared.

She took a hesitant step, then another, and stopped again. Which way?

But it was better to move in any direction than to stand here where Dagon's guards could grab her again.

She slid into the flow of people, let it carry her along as she edged to the other side of the street, sidestepped a donkey leading a rickety cart, and pushed across to creep along the row of homes that edged the street.

This must be the way. Would she find them there?

But then, suddenly, they found her.

"Zarah!"

There was Noah, surging toward her along the wall, arms reaching for her.

And Shem and Ham, following behind.

"We were about to go back in—"

She caught Noah's hands in her own. Relief mixed with dread flooded her heart.

He pulled her into his chest.

"Japheth? Salbeth?" She searched Noah's face, his eyes for answers.

"They are safe." He kissed the top of her head. "We will explain later. Come."

How could it have been so easy? She had expected a fight. At the very least, to sneak through the temple unseen in the late watches of the night, praying to go undetected. How could she have simply run through the front door?

Follow.

Yes, yes, she had followed. The One God had told her to follow Noah, and she had obeyed.

Run.

He had told her to run, and she had obeyed.

How much better to respond in obedience than to work in her own strength!

And now she followed and she ran once more, on the heels of Noah and her sons, back to the alley.

Quick embraces from all, with a longer squeeze of Salbeth, tears flowing on both sides. The girl was clearly weak, and she was bruised and dirty, but she was whole.

Japheth's hand—she would unwrap that dirty scrap of tunic later and tend to it—but for now he waved it off as though it were nothing.

And then they mounted, the six of them, emerged from the alley with heads down, urged their horses faster against the flow of people, toward the city gates.

Through the central hub of the city, past the main well.

The gates loomed ahead, closed at this hour.

Zarah prayed there would be someone to open them, to let them out.

They rode faster, clearing the crowds as they drew nearer the gate.

Zarah peered around Noah's shoulder from her place behind him on the horse. Yes, there was a keeper, standing in the center of the wide gate, facing them.

One of her sons was shouting to the gatekeeper to swing them open, but the man was not moving.

And then she knew.

"Dagon," she whispered against Noah's cheek. "Dagon stands at the gate!"

He held his priestly staff at his side, but as they approached he raised it like a spear.

No guards accompanied him. He must have thought himself equal to all of them, whether because of his connection to the moon god or from sheer arrogance.

"Stand aside!" Shem jumped to the ground.

His brothers joined him.

Noah brought his horse alongside his sons and reined him to a stop. "We are leaving, Dagon. You cannot have us. Not any of us."

Dagon was unsmiling, unmoving. "You think that Kish is so far away, but you have seen that my power reaches there. And the moon god's power is absolute." He tilted his head back and stared into the night sky. "Even now, Sin looks down on you with disfavor. Your ship will turn to ash. Your family will turn to dust. And the moon god will still reign in the sky."

Shem and Ham looked to their father, and Noah nodded.

The two stomped forward to the gate. Each grabbed an arm of the high priest, lifted him off his feet, and tossed him aside into the dirt.

Japheth unlatched the city gates and swung one of them wide.

Ham and Japheth mounted their horses while Shem stood over Dagon, looking like he would kill the man if he must.

And then a moment later, they were all mounted and riding, leaving Dagon in the dust behind them.

Her sons were whooping with victory as their horses raced into the night, but Zarah simply smiled and leaned her forehead against Noah's back, content to close her eyes and feel the wind in her hair.

They rode through the night, and Zarah dozed off and on. At one point, with the dampness of dew on her shoulders, she felt Noah pull her from the horse and whisper that they were stopping for just a short while.

How much longer until they reached home? How much longer until their home was no more?

When they were riding again, she tried to imagine a river wide enough to lift their ship. Kish had a river that ran along its eastern edge, where she had washed clothes for years and where her sons had learned to swim. But, the boys had told her at its deepest point, they could touch the muddy bottom with their toes.

What sort of river would flow through their field to carry away a ship as large as they had built?

When the first ashen light spilled across the horizon, she breathed in the air and tried to keep her eyes open. The day had dawned gray and dismal.

"How much longer?"

Noah smiled over his shoulder. "Only a few hours, I promise."

"How can you be so certain?"

"Trust me, woman."

She would trust him. But he had better be right. Her legs and back were telling her she couldn't ride much longer.

And Noah was right. Before the sun had reached its peak, the landscape grew familiar.

She sat upright now, trying to see over Noah's shoulder.

Would the ship be unharmed? Were Aris and Na'el safe? It was a question none of them had asked each other during this journey. They had each known that Salbeth must be rescued. Worries about what they left behind would do no good.

But Japheth and Ham were riding faster now, no doubt anxious to be sure their wives were safe.

When they rounded the last bend and the ship came into view, it took Zarah's breath away.

What a thing they had accomplished as a family! It stood tall and noble against the morning sky, and even from this distance on the road, she could see that animals still milled around the outside, as if they were here for the journey but not yet ready to board.

Well, they would have to board soon, if Methuselah's seven days were accurate.

Would the end of all things truly come by the end of this day?

And then she saw the people.

She had thought at first they were smaller animals. But no, a crowd of townspeople was clumped in the field as well. Her stomach clenched. Had they come to do more harm?

Noah must have seen them too. He was urging Hazir faster, following the pace of Ham and Japheth.

Shem clucked at his horse, and he and Salbeth brought up the rear.

The crowd of people must have seen them coming. They were moving as one toward the road.

And Na'el and Aris must have been watching from the rooftop, for two female figures were running toward them, ahead of the crowd.

They reached the women quickly, and Ham and Japheth both swung their wives up onto the horses' backs.

The family huddled in a tight circle.

"What is it?" Noah asked the women they'd left behind. "Have they attacked again?" His eyes were scanning the outline of the ship against the sky.

Aris shook her head and simply pointed. Beyond the field, the people, even beyond the ship.

Once again, as it had more than a week ago, a plume of blackness spewed from one of the distant mountains. The column grew like an upside-down tree, with black roots spreading outward at the top.

Zarah looked away from the fearful thing. If only she could hold every one of her family to her. Keep them all safe from whatever was to come.

But no, that was what the One God had promised to do.

"Come," Noah said. "It is time."

The other seven looked to him, not moving.

He nodded. "Yes. We have done all we can. It is time."

CHAPTER THIRTY-FIVE

There was nothing to be gathered from the house.

Aris and Na'el had known the time was short and had brought everything that morning, before the people had started leaking from the city to grumble against the blackening sky and the ship they blamed for everything. Even the chickens from behind the house, and Muti, her beloved sheep, were now inside.

The eight rode in on their four horses, slowly through the watching crowd.

The men each kept a hand on their blades, and the women kept their arms around their husbands.

It was a strange procession, with insults and mockery hurled at them as they moved through. But no one accosted them.

Was it still the hand of the One God that kept them safe?

Zarah was glad when Noah edged out in front of his sons, to part the crowd and to lead them in.

The animals had stopped arriving, it would seem. The only remaining animals seemed docile, but without a keeper, waiting for one of Noah's family to show them the way inside. The people would not have been so comfortable in spreading across their fields if there was danger still from claws and teeth.

Claws and teeth. Were they truly about to live in a ship with all those wild beasts?

It was not time to ask questions. It was still time to simply follow.

But it was not to be a completely peaceful entrance into their new home. When they were still only halfway across the field, a group of men ranged themselves in front of the entrance ramp. Several were armed with clubs, perhaps the rest with blades, and the set of their shoulders looked most unfriendly.

Zarah clutched Noah a bit tighter, and he kept Hazir moving toward the blockade.

It did not surprise her to see the obvious leader of the men.

When they were near enough for conversation, Noah held up an arm to stop his sons and pulled back on Hazir's reins.

"We want no trouble, Barsal."

The younger man cocked his head. "That is the problem, Noah. You don't understand that *you* are the trouble. You bring it upon all of us, and now you bring it upon yourself."

"I have brought nothing but a message of repentance, for those who would listen to the One God's offer of grace. But you would not have it." He lifted his voice to encompass as many as could hear. "And now, any trouble that befalls, you have only yourselves to blame."

Perhaps to this crowd, the words sounded harsh. But Zarah heard in Noah's voice all the heartbreak of one who believed he had failed his people and now must watch them suffer.

Please, God. Do not let Noah watch them suffer.

"Let us pass, Barsal."

Barsal and those with him did not move.

"We will fight you if we must, but of what use is it to bring injury upon yourself? Upon your sons? We will go and live in our ship. You will not see us again, of that you have my word. Put your fate, and ours, in the hands of whatever gods you worship, and let the gods decide."

They were so close. Only a breath away from the culmination of years of building and waiting, of fighting and hoping.

Barsal's hard face grew more pinched. But perhaps even he could see the wisdom in Noah's words.

He took a slow side step, then another. The men with him, his sons and others, followed suit, giving wide berth to the four horses and their riders.

Without even dismounting, the family of eight walked their horses slowly up the wooden ramp toward the bowels of the ship.

Zarah took in a final sweeping glance toward all they had known. Her home. Their fields. Grandfather's home. Even the city behind them. Would any of it be left, after what was to come?

I am bringing floodwaters to destroy all flesh.... These were the words of the Voice, the words that the One God had spoken to Noah years ago.

Aris and Na'el had kept embers burning in the clay fire pit at the end of the ship, near the sluice where the rainwater flowed into the ship-bottom cistern and where smoke could escape. The orange glow at the end of the ship, meager as it was, somehow felt comforting. A little bit of home, inside their wooden box.

They dismounted, led the horses to pens, and then ranged around the open doorway to face those who still stood in their field.

The remaining animals filed in, past where they stood, until their field held only people.

Had the sky grown darker as they were entering? Shadows seemed to fall upon the faces of those who watched. Perhaps it was only the smoky blackness of the sky above the mountains behind them.

But then there was a sound. Like the stampeding of horses across a field.

More animals?

She glanced at Noah. From the sound, it might be hundreds. Where would they put them?

But the crowd was not dispersing. It was shaking. Trembling.

No, the ground was trembling.

The stampede turned into a crack like thunder and a roar like a thousand wild lions.

"Close the door!" Shem was yelling, scrambling for the rope attached to the bottom end of the ramp.

Ham joined him.

Noah and Japheth snatched up the other rope.

A moment later all four women wrapped their hands around the ropes and heaved.

They had never tried to pull the ramp upward.

Never wondered if eight people could accomplish it.

And now it seemed they couldn't.

Outside the ship, the people of the city began to scream in terror. They darted to and fro, as if they could escape the shaking of the earth.

If only she could bring them all into the ship!

Would God relent? Were there others He would allow?

She pulled with all her strength, teeth gritted against the stinging scrape of the rope against her palms, but she watched for any friends, any neighbors, who would repent.

Fall on His mercy, friends!

Several were running for the ship!

She eased in her heaving of the rope. The ramp was partway closed. Should they lower it again? Allow these friends to join them?

Pale faces, terror-filled, just outside the ship...

"This is your fault!" A woman Zarah had never known shrieked and shook her fists. "Your doing! You have brought the sky down upon us! You and your God!"

Others began to yell. To accuse.

Zarah's heart broke.

Still, still they refused Him.

Like the sheep stealer who was only angry at those who punished his crimes, these people would refuse the grace of God until their very end.

The rope was slipping now.

Fatigue and brokenheartedness had rendered them all too exhausted to lift the ramp that would become the door.

I am bringing floodwaters....

What good was a ship in a flood, if the door was not closed?

The ramp dropped to the field with a massive thud, kicking up a cloud of dust. The people nearest to them jumped backward.

Zarah half expected them to rush into the ship and try to kill them all, but they only kept moving backward.

Noah yelled something to the family, but the noise outside the ship deafened her.

She shook her head and held out her hands to signal her lack of understanding.

Another crack like thunder.

More screams.

And then the ramp began to lift.

Were the townspeople closing them into their own ship? Did they think to seal them in and perhaps appease the wrath of their demon-gods?

No, no there were no hands pushing it upward, no angry faces yelling curses.

The ramp lifted as though pulled upward by an unseen force.

The family moved backward, grabbed each other's hands.

And the One God closed the door.

They stood a moment there together, hands clasped, feeling the shock of the sudden muffling of the chaos outside, the near-total darkness.

Noah broke from the family cluster first. "Tie the ropes!"

Her sons joined him, grabbing at the lead ropes that dangled from the top corners of the ramp-turned-door.

Her eyes were barely adjusted to the dim light. The men worked to secure the ropes to the posts they had fashioned for the purpose.

She and the other women still huddled together, unspeaking.

They could no longer hear voices outside. The ship's walls were too thick. But the earth still rumbled and heaved.

The men finished, and as a group they moved toward the end of the ship, seeking the comfort of the glowing embers. They sat in a circle, wordless.

Once, many years ago, Zarah had set a large clay jug on the wall surrounding the rooftop of their house. A few minutes later she bumped against it, and sent it tumbling over the edge. It hit the lip of the rain barrel beside the house. The sound of that clay jug exploding, shattering into fragments…that was the sound that the earth now made. It was as if they all hid inside the rain barrel, while the clay earth shattered around them.

And then a new sound…the patter of a hundred thousand drumbeats against the top of the ship.

Rain.

"I am going above." Noah stood as he spoke.

She grabbed at the hem of his tunic. "Don't."

He shook his head. "I must see. I must."

There was no arguing with Noah when he got that sharp hardness in his voice, so she let him go.

And then they all followed.

Up the ramp to the middle deck, then the upper, and finally climbing the ladder that led to the roof of their new home.

They emerged into the pounding rain, one by one.

Zarah held her forearm partly over her eyes. She scanned the horizon, noting more than one plume of black smoke through the rain.

And something else, something never seen if her eyes could be trusted.

Just as the inky black flowed upward from the mountain ridges, in other places it seemed that water gushed upward from cracks in the surface of the land.

How could such a thing be?

She glanced toward their field, toward the city. Thankfully, the people had scattered, probably when the rain started. They would be in their homes when the floods came....

She forced the thought from her mind and went back to the ladder, back down into the ship.

Minutes later, they had all exchanged wet tunics for dry and were back at the fire again.

Zarah poked at the embers and fed more fuel, trying to ward off the chill of the rain and the sadness.

Salbeth brought bread and wine. They passed the loaf, each tearing a piece, and then the wineskin, sharing the simple meal in silence.

Zarah leaned her head against Noah's shoulder and closed her eyes.

Noah finally spoke. "All these years, building this ark. I have needed much faith to trust in the words of the One God who told me to build it." He looked around their family circle. "And you have needed faith, in both the One God and in me." He squeezed Zarah's hand. "But now, now is the time that our faith is truly tested. Even though we have seen what God warned has come to pass—*is* coming to pass—we now must trust that His ways are good. That despite the destruction, He is just. That although we are all who will soon be left, He is merciful."

Zarah nodded and took a deep breath. "His ways are not our ways. But He will always make a way."

Noah pulled her close and kissed her cheek.

He smelled of bread and wine, and somehow the moment felt sacred.

"Yes," he said. "He will always make a way."

EPILOGUE

One Year Later

Kick it!"

Zarah's shout surprised them all.

The stubborn door to the ship remained lodged closed, as it had been for the long months they had spent inside.

But today! Today the dove had not returned. Today the One God had told Noah it was time.

Now they stood awaiting their freedom, and the door to the ship would not open!

Laughing, the four men kicked the stubborn wood.

With a squeal and a crack, it tore from its socket. Sunlight poured in through the widening gap.

And then the wooden door fell.

Zarah had never been so happy to see mud in all her life.

It had been a long year, one they could not have imagined when they were tasked with building this floating box.

They had not brought nearly enough food, never envisioning that they would be confined so long. And so as the months dragged on, they first had to eat some of the food brought for animals, and then even some of the animals themselves had become food for them, and for the other species. Surely this was part of the reason that God had instructed them to take more of the clean animals.

And they could not have envisioned the delicate balance of all the living things upon the ship, from the smallest of insects that were discovered as time went on, to the largest of mammals that required so much care. Thankfully, the cisterns in the bottom of the ship had collected water as it rained, and they had never thirsted.

But there were days when they despaired of ever leaving. Days when they argued and yelled and sought the corners of the ship to be alone.

And other days, when they had laughed and rested and simply expressed thankfulness.

Now at last they stood on the threshold, getting their first look at the world washed clean.

Zarah breathed in the damp air, lifted her face to the sunshine.

Methuselah would have loved this.

The old man had always known, always told them that the One God was working toward restoration, desiring the cleansing and healing of broken humanity. That He would ensure His sovereign plan continued, and never be thwarted by the sin and corruption of people or even of demons.

And now Na'el, Aris, and Salbeth stood beside their husbands, each one carrying in her womb the next generation.

Yes, an eventful year.

Noah smiled at his family and extended his hand toward the green outdoors.

The next step would be a big one, for all of them.

They would first build an altar, of course, and offer sacrifices to God. But after that... After that, they must find a way to build a new world.

A daunting task. But when had that stopped them?

She returned Noah's smile, and was the first to take a step off the ship into this new world.

She would not be afraid. This was God's plan, and she was only called to simple and faithful obedience with what she had been given. No one was too old, too broken, or too far gone for redemption, and no one was worthless in God's eyes. He was willing to use ordinary and even damaged people, those willing to take dramatic, faith-filled, and courageous steps forward.

It was never too late to begin again.

* * *

FACTS BEHIND
the Fiction

◆

A VERY ABLE HELPMATE

It's hard to know what life was like for Noah's wife, or Zarah, as she is called in this story, and her daughters-in-law. We can't even be sure in what millennia they lived. But, regardless of when she lived, we can surmise she worked hard.

Some students of the Bible meticulously calculate every generation reported in the Bible and then come up with a date of somewhere around 4500 BC. Other scholars, however, say the genealogies in the Bible are intended to be highlights of human history and that there were many other generations unreported, which would push the date much further back. At the very least, if the numbers are complete as is, these women lived in what the archaeologists call the Stone Age. If archaeologists are correctly interpreting evidence they found from Neolithic times, Noah lived about the time many say the Stone Age started to give way to the Bronze Age.

Researchers from universities in Cambridge, Vienna, and Canada studied and CT-scanned the bones of Neolithic women. Writing in a journal called *Science Advances*, they said the women's arms were more than ten percent stronger than those of women on the Cambridge University rowing team. So, apparently, training twice a day and rowing 75 miles (120 km) a week can't match the muscle power it

HAND GRAIN GRINDER

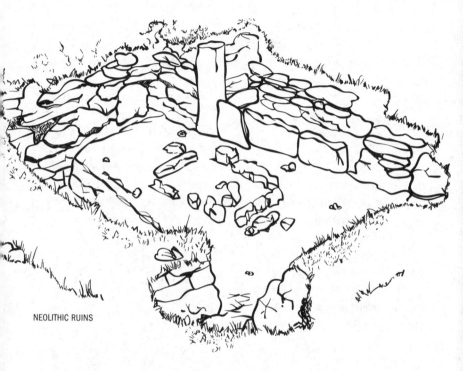

NEOLITHIC RUINS

takes to hand grind grain into flour for half a day and then work in the fields and do other chores until sundown.

Researchers explain that strong muscles build bigger bones since bone is living tissue. The size of the prehistoric bones provided clues to the power in the muscles.

Some archaeologists, studying Stone Age ruins from when some calculate that Noah lived, report that the evidence points to everyone in the family pulling together to survive. Men and women both gathered plants. Both hunted too, and provided for their families.

With that in mind, it is not difficult to imagine Zarah, the First Lady of the Ark, working alongside Noah and their sons in the boat-building project.

LONGEVITY OF BIBLICAL PROPORTIONS

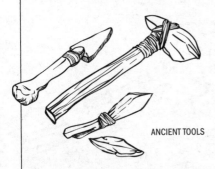

ANCIENT TOOLS

Before the Great Flood, people lived longer than we do—centuries longer, according to Genesis. Born before the Great Flood, Adam lived 930 years, Noah 950, and the Bible's record holder, Methuselah, 969.

But by the time of Noah, ten generations into the human race, the Genesis writer says God was thoroughly disappointed with humanity. God decided not only to wash the planet clean for a fresh start, He dramatically reduced the human lifespan. "No one will live for more than one hundred twenty years" (Genesis 6:3 CEV).

After the Flood, the numbers began to drop off sharply. Noah's son Shem was born before the flood and lived to be about 600 years old (Genesis 11:10–11). But Abraham, born after the Flood, lived 175 years (Genesis 25:7–8). Moses lived 120 years (Deuteronomy 34:7) and David lived seventy years (2 Samuel 5:4, 1 Kings 2:10–11).

Extreme lifespans that stretched into centuries seem unbelievable today. If people lived as long as Methuselah did, Richard the Lionheart (1157–1199) might still be here to tell us about the Crusades. Better than that, we might be just two long lifetimes away from an eyewitness to the ministry of Jesus Christ.

AN ANCIENT CLAY PRISM WITH A LIST OF SUMERIAN KINGS

Accounts of incredibly long lifespans show up outside the Bible too. The combined lifespans of eight Sumerian kings who ruled before the Flood stretched into nearly a quarter of a million years. That's according to a 4,000-year-old clay prism from the world's first known civilization, located in what is now south Iraq. The shortest reign lasted 18,600 years.

Why were the ages reported in the Bible so high before the Flood? Some speculate that the Flood altered the environment, perhaps dissipating thick clouds that protected people from harmful radiation. Or maybe underground water roaring up to join the Flood tore loose previously dormant toxins from the ground.

THE DOVE: A SYMBOL OF PEACE

Noah took aboard the ark "seven pairs of every kind of animal that can be used for sacrifice and one pair of all others" (Genesis 7:2 CEV).

After the flood rains stopped, Noah waited several months for the waters to recede enough for him to disembark with his family and all God's creatures.

He sent birds to scout for dry land. When a dove came back carrying a green leaf from an olive tree, Noah knew the floodwaters were starting to drop. Three months later he threw open the doors for everyone to leave the ark that had protected them for more than a year.

Today, pictures of a dove carrying an olive branch symbolize peace. However, it was likely not Noah but the early Christians—with the help of ancient Greek and Roman writers—who developed and promoted the idea that a dove holding an olive branch represented peace.

The Roman poet Virgil used an olive branch to represent peace in a scene from his masterpiece poem *Aeneid*, written in about 20 BC. The poem featured a Trojan named Aeneas, who held "an olive branch in

EARLY CHRISTIAN DOVE,
CATACOMB OF SAN SEBASTIANO, ROME

his hand" while delivering the message, "The Trojans and their chief bring holy peace."

Christians later linked the image of the Holy Spirit descending like a dove at the baptism of Jesus to this established image of peace. Early Christian art chiseled into the stone walls of the catacombs in Rome include a picture of a dove holding an olive branch.

A Christian scholar from North Africa, Tertullian (about AD 160–220), eventually pulled Noah's story into the emerging symbolism. He said that just as Noah's dove represented peace, by announcing the end of divine punishment of the world, the Holy Spirit descending like a dove "brought us the peace of God, sent from heaven" (*Writings of Tertullian*, volume 3, chapter 8).

WHY NOT JUST CALL IT A BOAT?

Noah built what sounds like a floating warehouse half as wide as a football field and long enough to stretch deep into both end zones.

It's one of a kind in the Bible. And it gets a rare Hebrew word to describe it, variously translated as *tevat, tebah, teba*. Attaching English letters to Hebrew so we can pronounce the word isn't always an exact science. But scholars try to get us in the ballpark.

When it came time to translate the Hebrew word into English for the King James Version of the Bible, the king's scholars called it an "ark." More recent Bible versions call it a boat.

In all the Bible, this unique Hebrew word shows up in only one other story—the floating baby Moses. It describes the papyrus reed basket that his mother made and waterproofed. She put him inside the tiny ark and set it along the banks of the Nile River near where a princess bathed.

Scholars can only guess where the word came from. One guess is that it was borrowed from Egypt, where Moses grew up and probably studied in the royal palace. That might suggest this was the original word because there's no evidence Moses lived long enough to learn the Hebrew language of the Jews. Some say Moses lived in the 1400s BC. Others say 1200s BC. But the Hebrew language didn't seem to branch off from the similar Canaanite language until around 1000 BC, when Bible writers report that the Jews were getting settled in the land.

The book of Genesis, credited by many scholars to have been authored by Moses, might well have been written in some form of Egyptian or another language. In that case, scribes would have later translated it into Hebrew, but they kept the original Egyptian word for *ark*.

Surprisingly, the Hebrew term describing the ark that held the Ten Commandments comes from a different word entirely. It's a word that refers to a container such as a "box" or "chest."

Perhaps the big question about the Hebrew word for Noah's ark is why it deserved such a unique term. Why not just call it a boat? Perhaps the unique word from the mouth and the writings of Moses seemed appropriate when describing the boat that saved humanity and the basket that saved the man who would organize Israel into a nation ruled by God's laws.

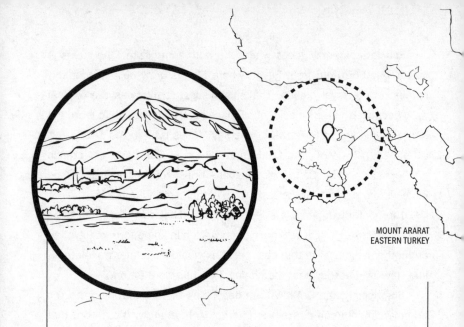

MOUNT ARARAT
EASTERN TURKEY

WHERE TO PARK AN ARK:
ARARAT MOUNTAINS

In the seventh month of the year, Noah's ark ran aground
"somewhere in the Ararat mountains" (Genesis 8:4 CEV).

The Genesis writer may have meant what is today called the Armenian Highlands in eastern Turkey, a mountain range crowned by its highest peak: Mount Ararat.

Ararat is a dormant volcano that pushed itself three miles (five km) into the sky. That's an altitude of nearly 17,000 feet (5,200 m).

This mountain range covers a land mass almost half that of the Rocky Mountains—American and Canadian. At about 150,000 square miles (400,000 square km), the Armenian Highlands are nearly as big as California.

Turkish locals call Mount Ararat *Ağrı Dağı,* "Pain Mountain." For at least the past thousand years, locals have claimed this as the landing spot of Noah's ark.

Their stories lured many explorers to Ararat, including astronaut James Irwin, who walked on the moon during the *Apollo 15* mission. Teams climbed Mount Ararat, searching for remnants of the grounded ark.

So far, though plenty of unproven sightings have been reported, along with some hoaxes, no solid evidence has presented itself.

French explorer Fernand Navarra produced a hand-cut beam he said he found locked in ice two miles (3 km) up the mountain. It tested only about 1,200 years old—some 3,000 years short. Worse, his guide later confessed that Navarra carried the beam up the mountain and back down.

Mount Ararat might have been the first peak in the Highlands to surface after the Flood dissipated, but it was not the only possible parking space in the sprawling mountain range. Yet, while there is much about the life and times of Noah and his family that we don't know, of this we can be certain: God can take just one obedient life out of a sinful and rebellious world and, through him or her, bring redemption and a fresh start.

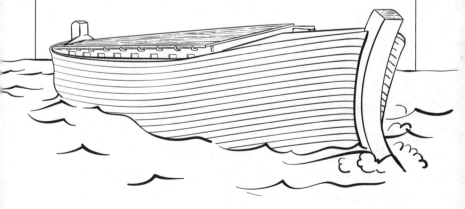

Fiction Author
TRACY L. HIGLEY

Tracy is a prolific author, having written over a dozen historical novels and nonfiction books. Her love of the biblical stories led her to a master's degree in ancient and classical history, and that learning, combined with her extensive travels through Europe and the Middle East, gives flavor and authenticity to the historical novels she sets in exotic times and places like ancient Egypt, Rome, and Greece. She can be found online at tracyhigley.com.

Nonfiction Author
STEPHEN M. MILLER

Stephen M. Miller is an award-winning, bestselling Christian author of easy-reading books about the Bible and Christianity. His books have sold over 1.9 million copies and include *The Complete Guide to the Bible, Who's Who and Where's Where in the Bible,* and *How to Get into the Bible.*

Miller lives in the suburbs of Kansas City with his wife, Linda, a registered nurse. They have two married children who live nearby.

Read on for a sneak peek of another exciting story
in the Ordinary Women of the Bible series!

AN UNLIKELY WITNESS: JOANNA'S STORY

by Ginger Garrett

The Month of Adar, 29 CE
Inside the Palace of Herod Antipas, in Tiberius

Alone with her husband in his chamber, Joanna watched him prepare for his journey. Misery clutched at her heart.

"You were patient with me in the beginning," she reminded Chuza. "Kind."

"I delighted in you." He sighed. The words lingered in the air between them. They were true words. Chuza had delighted in her, but those days were over.

"When will you return?" She sat upon a bench next to the dressing table. A servant watched the couple from lowered eyes, pretending not to listen. Joanna didn't care any longer. It was hard to hold on to dignity in Herod Antipas's palace. It was hard to hold on to anything.

"When my business is done," he answered.

She winced slightly. She knew why he had chosen this date to leave. Shaking her head slightly to clear her mind, she decided she would have to think about that later. Perhaps she would walk in the gardens when he left.

He looked away. "Herod wants me to prepare the Black Fortress."

"Machaerus?" She gasped. "Does he anticipate war?" Machaerus was a military fortress, known also as the Black Fortress, elevated high in the mountains on the eastern edge of the Dead Sea. On a clear day, you could see Masada, Jerusalem, Alexandrium, even Cypros. On holy days, you could see the smoke from the fires at the temple in Jerusalem. No one vacationed at Machaerus, though. It was built by Herod the Great for defense of the kingdom.

"John the Baptizer has been spotted in that region," Chuza murmured, as if that was an explanation.

This man named John had been stirring up the people, especially her own people, the Jews.

Chuza walked to a table to review a collection of scrolls. He lifted one at a time, inspecting the seals. "Herod will travel there with the court. He very much wants to hear this man speak."

Why did not Herod command John to appear in Tiberius, then? It made no sense. Joanna started to protest. A sudden, terrible idea occurred. "Do you go to see a woman?"

He shook his head, but his back was turned. She had no way to read his expression.

"Go, then," she said softly. "I have no way to secure you."

"You did not need a way, once." Regret colored his voice.

"You did not seek to leave me, once." She gathered her frightened, exhausted thoughts and found the courage to press him for the truth. "Is it because you do not love me anymore? Or is it because you have grown tired of me? Of my infirmity?"

"No!" Turning, he crossed the room, his hands extended as if to take her in his arms again.

Her breath caught in her chest. He stopped just before he reached her, dropping his hands to his side, looking away.

"The shame is too great," he whispered. "If I lost my place at Herod's side, we would both be lost, Joanna. You cannot go back to your family. I cannot provide without Herod. But I have to prove that I am a man worthy of my title."

Chuza was the palace steward for Herod Antipas, in charge of all financial operations and procurements. Chuza got people what they wanted. That was his job, and he was good at it. If Herod wanted building supplies, a rare wood or the purest gold, Chuza got it. If a nobleman needed safe passage to another country for a private trade, Chuza made it happen. The world was an open market to Chuza. Nothing was denied him, and Herod took pains to be sure Chuza was well rewarded. Chuza could have anything in the world, and he could usually arrange to have it delivered too. No one argued or disagreed with him. No one could.

Joanna smiled wistfully at the bitter irony. She too had never disagreed or argued with him. Yet she could not give him what he most wanted, what he needed as a noble in this palace—an heir.

The next morning, she sought refuge in the green of the garden. Joanna emerged from the shadows of the palace into the bright sun, intent on stealing a few moments alone in the royal gardens of Herod Antipas, son of the late Herod the Great. To walk in the quiet gardens offered something that neither Rome nor ruler could grant. Peace.

The gardens here in Tiberius had become a refuge for her. She had been raised in a busy village, so she wondered why the quiet gardens held such a special place in her heart. She had also been raised a Jew, so she should have yearned for the temple courts in Jerusalem, perhaps, or a synagogue. In her family, however, religion was used for climbing the social ladder, not digging into spiritual depths. So her love of gardens really made no sense at all, but it was a pleasant mystery she had no plans to solve.

The bright sun warmed her skin as she paused at the garden's entrance. She took a moment to relish the light.

Sighing, she tilted her face to the sun, letting the rays caress her cheeks. Today she celebrated ten years of marriage. She celebrated alone, as was fitting. Barren, she had been unable to give her husband what he most wanted—a child. Ambitious, he had been unable to give her what she most wanted—love.

Inhaling deeply, she caught the scent of a storm moving in. She needed to hurry, or she might miss her chance to relax.

She walked down the path, grateful to be free of the thick incense of Herodias's chambers. Herodias would be bitter company today. Herodias expected less important women to share entertaining gossip or information useful to the rich and powerful. Joanna trafficked in neither.

Joanna knew that this was seen as a character flaw, even though Herodias was a Jew, and the women should have shared the same values. Herodias was not just a Jew, though. She was a royal, a princess from the Hasmonean line. Herodias was also married to Herod Antipas, son of Herod the Great. When Herod Antipas married her, it had given him a distinct political edge over his brothers. He married into royalty. He should naturally, then, rule over the majority of their father's kingdom. After all, Rome liked keeping the Jewish citizens content. A Jewish princess certainly could help do that.

But any hope of Herodias becoming a queen had been dashed by that cruel old tyrant, Herod the Great. As death drew near to the gates for Herod the Great, the venom that ran in the old king's veins spewed out onto his sons. By the time his body was cold, three sons divided the kingdom that remained.

Now Herod Antipas ruled over a land that was one fourth the size of his father's original kingdom. Herod Antipas was only a tetrarch, "a ruler of a quarter," and not a king. His brother, Archelaus, had ruled over half, until he'd been exiled because the Jews hated him. A man named Pontus Pilate ruled in his place, appointed by Rome.

A second brother, Philip, also ruled over one quarter. Augustus Caesar supervised both remaining brothers and reminded them regularly that their power ultimately came from Rome.

And so, Herod Antipas did not get what he most wanted, and neither did Herodias. He was not a king and so Herodias was not a queen. She was just one more woman who had married for power and woke up with a bureaucracy.

Joanna stretched for a moment, trying to remember why she had sought the gardens.

Just ahead, a grove of almond trees lined the path. Spring was not quite here yet but winter had loosened its grip. This month, the month of Adar, was a month of extremes. The almond trees were heavy with white and pink blooms. Storms could destroy them in an instant, but Joanna hoped the month would be gentle. In the month of Adar, she was always tempted to count the blooms when she walked in the gardens. She wanted to protect each one, somehow, from the harsh storms that could descend in an instant. She wanted every blossom to become a thick cluster of almonds. She loved that.

On her right, guards straightened their posture as she approached. She nodded and smiled. They visibly relaxed and nodded back.

She didn't believe in magic, though Herod Antipas had plenty of court magicians. She believed in the one true God that the rabbis spoke of. She just wished this God wasn't so cold, so stern and hard to please, the way they described Him, because when she walked in the gardens she wanted more than anything to clap her hands and exclaim that He had done a marvelous trick, turning flowers into almonds, right under her nose!

Of course, if she could talk to God, she would have other things to discuss.

A gardener emerged from a row of trees, carrying a basket of twine. He was accustomed to her daily strolls in the garden and nodded in greeting. Perhaps she should have insisted on more formal greetings from the staff, but she was not a royal. She was only a wife. Her only job was childbearing. Her father's dowry had bought her into this palace, and she had failed in the one thing she had to do to stay.

Ten years married now and no children. Why did her thoughts come back to that problem, always? She had meant to enjoy a moment of peace out here and could think of only her troubles.

She'd done all that the royal physicians, here and in Rome, had recommended. She'd eaten pomegranates until her fingers were stained red, she'd drunk strange herbs until her head swam with visions, she'd bathed in rivers and prayed in the three watches of the night. Just to be sure, she'd prayed again on other nights in the four watches of the Romans. As a Jew, she marked time differently than the Roman Empire did. Rome hated that, just as Rome hated that Jews used a different calendar and celebrated different festivals. Rome preferred one calendar, one way of telling time. Which was efficient, and Chuza loved the idea. But efficient was not to be confused with moral, and Rome was not confused about morals. It had none.

But, after ten years, she was so tired of hearing so much disdain from Rome about her God that she finally decided to offer up a few prayers to their gods, using one of their sundials to mark time. If a Roman official tried to offer Chuza advice about childbearing, at least Chuza could say that the Roman gods had been appeased. Even if none of the officials knew which god was on duty or when.

She shook her head. This had to stop. This was an afternoon to be enjoyed. A rare moment of peace in a palace of strife. A storm was coming, and she would be driven back inside, trapped with Herodias for hours.

Walking along the manicured path that led through the gardens, she ducked behind an almond tree and removed her slippers. The dirt here was combed daily so that not even a stone could harm Herod. She loved the feel of the cool earth under her feet, sensing the gentle slope of a tree root beneath the ground, searching in the darkness for water. Overhead, the branches sprang to life with delicate white blossoms, each with a pool of bright pinkish-red at the center. The trees were displays of extravagance, with hundreds of blossoms, the white petals too blindingly pure to be so close to the saturated red and pink centers, yet the artistry of each remained perfect. No human hand could paint thousands of blossoms like this without smudging or ruining at least one. The capacity for repetition, for perfection and beauty in each new blossom, was a marvel. She walked along the path, watching the sunlight filter through the branches laced with blossoms, and the light play upon her skin. Soon the blossoms would fall, only to be replaced with the fruit that would be the almond.

She would miss the blossoms, though. Each season brought such beauty. A rumble of thunder caught her attention. She reached out to touch a soft blossom, hoping the storm would not shake too many free.

Rabbis taught that the blooms symbolized that God was always watching to see His Word fulfilled, yet as Joanna surveyed the Jews walking along dusty roads beneath the palace, she wondered if God saw what she did. Herod Antipas was not a friend of the Jews. Indeed, he was a friend to no one, only because he tried so hard to be a friend to everyone. His father, Herod the Great, had been so notoriously evil that his son Herod Antipas had wanted to be known for something else entirely. And he was. Herod Antipas was known for marrying his half-brother's wife. Who was also Antipas's niece.

The Herods were a complicated, immoral bunch. Immorality was usually that way, she had noticed. Both father and son had wanted to be thought of as Jewish leaders, but in their hearts, they were Romans. They served under a Roman Caesar, and in Rome's name they ruled.

At least the son had tried to undo some of the damage his father had done to the Jews. Herod Antipas had dedicated his life to building cities, not tearing them apart. His great building project, the city of Tiberius, had started as a disaster, however, another casualty of not quite understanding the Jews.

He had chosen to build the city on top of an ancient Jewish settlement, which included a cemetery. No Jew wanted to break ground over the dead bodies of their ancestors. This violated the law of cleanliness. Herod had paid dearly with imported laborers and bribes before the city had begun to take shape.

She didn't know—perhaps no one did—what he had done with the bodies. Perhaps they were still in the ground.

Joanna watched the people trudging along the roads beneath the palace gardens. How many of them knew the truth about this city, this palace, this ruler?

Would God intervene one day to set things right for them? For her? She waited for an answer to her prayers, just as they did.

All the Jews waited for a rumored savior that had never arrived. Centuries ago, the birth of a great king, the King of the Jews, had been foretold. A few decades ago, Herod the Great had commanded that every male child under two be met with the sword. He was determined to cancel the prophecy of a savior born to the people.

Apparently, he had succeeded. No one had arisen to save the Jews. No government had formed to challenge Rome. Herod the Great had died old, fat, and wealthy. They said it was a mysterious disease that claimed his life.

Joanna scoffed at the idea. Herod had cheated death hundreds of times, perhaps thousands. There was no mystery in his death, only that such an evil man had been allowed to live and prosper undisturbed for so many years.

So many mothers had wept for sons lost, maybe some of these same women walking the roads in the city below. In the beginning of the construction work, there hadn't been any Jews in the city, but now they traded here freely.

Below, a lone woman paused and seemed to cast a dark glance up at the palace. Joanna wondered what the woman had lost. The palace cast a shadow over the city, the homes, the stalls at the market, and everyone's lives. The palace took a portion of everyone's earnings, even children's, and they could not refuse to pay the tax.

Nothing had ever been denied to the men who wore the crown and the seal of Herod.

Her breath caught in her throat. A quick movement among the trees caught her eye. She stilled herself, holding her breath, listening for a clue as to who else was in the garden with her. After a moment, whispers reached her ears. She heard a man's voice, harsh and low. He was angry. Next, she heard a girl's voice, high and breathless, answering him when he paused long enough for her to reply.

After several moments, Joanna gathered the hem of her robe in her hand and checked to be sure her shawl was draped correctly with its broach identifying her as the wife of an important official. She walked down the center of the path, searching for the couple.

Though Joanna only saw his back, his rank was easy enough to identify. The straps across his back from the bronze chest piece and his thick leather belt made it clear he was a palace guard, probably a hired Gentile mercenary.

The soldier had a young servant girl cornered and cowering against a tree. The girl's face was red from tears.

"I did not mean to make a promise." The girl wept.

"You will honor your word, or I will make sure you have no honor left!" he snapped.

"What goes on here?" Joanna demanded.